SHADOWS OF MY FUTURE SELF

NINA REID

LUMINARE PRESS
WWW.LUMINAREPRESS.COM

Shadows of My Future Self
Copyright © 2023 by Nina Reid

All rights reserved. This book or any portion thereof may not be reproduced or used in any manner whatsoever without the express written permission of the publisher, except for the use of brief quotations in a book review.

Printed in the United States of America

Luminare Press
442 Charnelton St.
Eugene, OR 97401
www.luminarepress.com

LCCN: 2023900419
ISBN: 979-8-88679-134-1

Dedicated to my husband, my colleagues and clients, and my family and friends, near and far.

Contents

Prologue   1

CHAPTER 1
Eighteen Years in a Nutshell   5

CHAPTER 2
From Voltaire to Au Pair   17

CHAPTER 3
The French Disconnection   35

CHAPTER 4
Planes, Trains, and Couch Surfing   47

CHAPTER 5
First, Take My Money; Then Burst My Bubble   55

CHAPTER 6
Egomania   59

CHAPTER 7
A Process of Elimination   63

CHAPTER 8
Hyphens, Italics, and Commas—Oh, My!   73

CHAPTER 9
OT Doesn't Mean Overtime, But It Was About Time   81

CHAPTER 10
From Shadow to Light   87

CHAPTER 11
Pithy Takeaways   95

CHAPTER 12
Final Takeaways, Frenchy Style OR You Can Take the Girl Out of the French Lit, But You Can't Take the French Lit Out of the Girl   99

Acknowledgments   103
About the Author   105

Author Note: The following narrative depicts actual events and people within a real timeline to the best of the author's memory. Some artistic license was used in Chapter 9 in the depiction of the student encounters. Most identifying information such as names of people and places have either been altered or omitted for the privacy of those involved. One notable exception is the name/location of the author's undergraduate university.

Prologue

It is a warm afternoon in mid-May, almost three o'clock, and a gentle breeze finds its way through the open window of the empty preschool room where I've set up camp for the last hour. I'm sitting on a grown-up chair, hunched over a tot-sized table. I take a deep breath, enjoying the fresh air and welcome silence, gathering my thoughts after a hectic day. (The preschoolers are out early today, and the teacher, who is meeting with a colleague down the hall, is always generous in sharing her space with me and the other itinerant staff in her classroom.) I'd hoped to get out the door by three and hit the gym, but four o'clock now seems more likely. There's an evaluation report to finish writing on a fifth grader—due to be emailed to the parents first thing in the morning with the psychologist's report, and an email to send to another parent, Mrs. Garza, about home activities she can do with her daughter while she's in quarantine.

Pausing to look at my weekly planner, I reflect on the day. "Wow," I think to myself, "between individual and group treatments, I've seen ten kids today." Most of the sessions went well, except for the kindergarten student who lost it—screamed and threw his backpack—when he couldn't find his favorite water bottle. The social worker and I calmed down him down by coaxing him to go to the classroom "cozy corner" with playdough and reassurances that his water bottle was safe at home—his mom just forgot to pack it. With some encouragement, he took a few deep breaths and agreed that he'd use a plastic cup for the day. Then there was the first grader who refused to leave class and follow me to the sensory room because it housed the "scary and loud" magnetic timer. I showed her the silent duck timer on my phone (a picture of a duck gradually reveals itself—when the image is complete, time's up). After a few more refusals, she relented and joined me in the sensory room to practice calming yoga poses and use the platform swing. I even snuck in a quick handwriting activity before the duck bounced around on my phone in perfect formation, signaling it was time to return to the classroom. The highlight of the day was when one of the morning preschoolers, a quiet, shy child hesitant to participate in crafts and messy play, cracked a wide smile when he saw the little cups of glitter glue in red, yellow, green, and blue. He murmured, "I love blue," and cautiously—but independently—dipped his cotton ball in the blue, gooey substance and dabbed it onto the coloring sheet, just as I had shown him. A simple image of a cartoon robot holding (inexplicably) a kite immediately became more vibrant with the four-year-old's efforts.

    I find I have a special affinity for the quieter children on my caseload—I was a quiet, shy kid myself. They can be easily overlooked and overshadowed by the more extroverted children, as well as children with behavior problems, who demand a lot of adult attention. Because of this, I appreciate the prominent role social workers play in most American schools today, unlike when I was a kid. It can only benefit kids to have social workers run groups at least at the early elementary level, and have eyes on all the children, to lessen the chance the more vulnerable kids will fall through the cracks. Turning back to my Chromebook, I glance at the time. I sigh to myself, "It's been a long day, but I need to forge ahead. The gym can wait until tomorrow." I then recall with relief that my husband and I have leftovers in the fridge—no need to stress about fixing dinner. A faint scent of sulfur enters my nostrils. Two years after having a mild case of COVID-19, I still intermittently encounter weird sulfur smells, often during times of stress. I remind myself that a hard day in this profession is infinitely better than a good day at any of my previous jobs, most which feel like a lifetime ago.

My phone vibrates and I glance down. It's a text message from Winnie, a longtime friend from one of those past lives. She's a French teacher in the south Chicago suburbs. I haven't seen her in ages, but we keep in touch. She asks, "Hey, when does your summer break start? I have two more weeks. Counting the days! We should hang out sometime in June." I smile. "Sounds like a plan," I think. But first, I need to focus on this email I promised Mrs. G, and the evaluation report that's only half-finished. Winnie's text can wait. I'll look forward to making plans with her in the coming days when I'm less distracted. Friends for three decades, we can wait three more days to connect.

Later that night, loading the dishwasher and wiping down the kitchen counters, my thoughts return to the more vulnerable children on my caseload, and I wonder about their home life. There's the first grader with autism who falls asleep at least once a week before 10:00 a.m. and is late much of the time. I know his parents are separated, and they share custody; the routines are probably different between the two households. What else is going on? Then there's the second grader who comes to school disheveled, often forgetting her Chromebook charger and other everyday school materials, like her writing and math folders. There's obviously a lot we don't see as professionals working with kids in the school system. Even the best-intentioned parents benefit from occasional guidance, and often they are understandably overwhelmed with other concerns—health issues, finances, spousal conflicts, you name it—that impact their child's life.

The kitchen clean (well, clean enough), I pick out some non-wrinkled clothes for the next day and pop a melatonin—not a nightly ritual but an occasional option when stress threatens a good night's sleep. My husband is still in the basement tinkering with something at his workbench, but I'm exhausted. I crawl into bed with a magazine. My thoughts involuntarily drift back to my own experiences as a kid, which, I believe, have drawn me toward my current profession, like a silent, strong undercurrent propelling me forward. And I wonder what would have happened if I'd gone to a larger high school like some of my Chicago-area friends? Would I have found a niche sooner?

I finally turn off the light and nod off. I have strange dreams where work-related issues interweave with childhood memories. I awake the next morning to my alarm clock, disoriented, as if jetlagged by my dream-induced time travel.

CHAPTER 1

Eighteen Years in a Nutshell

The sinuous, rocky path of my early adulthood can be traced to the usual culprit—early formative experiences. Looking in from the outside, I had everything growing up. Two educated parents. A comfortable middle-class home. My many happy memories include abundant Christmases, jubilant celebrations at birthdays and graduations, and even a few memorable family vacations.

The truth is, pain and joy often coexist. Delving into the first does not nullify the second. Parsing out some of the specific family dynamics of my childhood just helps readers better understand the seemingly poor judgment plaguing my life experiences early on. Not one to enjoy reading drawn-out descriptions of childhood woes, I will attempt to be succinct while highlighting the relevant details. OK. Let's start cracking that nut.

GENERATION GAP

My mother was born in the 1930s, long before the women's liberation movement began seriously percolating in the

'70s. The lifestyle options for many women of her generation were limited to housewife, nurse, or teacher. Women and girls were considered the weaker sex. Based on that mindset alone, as the only girl and younger child (I had just one older brother), I must have seemed very fragile to her.

On top of that, every decade brings with it some form of social and political strife that spreads generalized anxiety. In the 2020s, Americans face COVID-19, a hostile political rhetoric across a divided nation, and shocking news of police brutality against George Floyd, Breonna Taylor, and other black Americans. I was born in 1971, not long after the turbulent and violent 1960s, witness to political assassinations and civil rights unrest. Many horrors also unfolded during the '70s—enough to trigger or exacerbate a mother's anxiety. This was the decade of several notorious serial killers, such as Ted Bundy and John Wayne Gacy, preceded by the Manson killings in 1969—scary stuff for a new parent to witness, process, and hold in her subconscious. I can only speculate that this backdrop reinforced her fear that the world was a dangerous place for her only daughter.

METAPHORICAL BUBBLE WRAP

When I was a baby, I imagine my mother, like most parents, went to great lengths to babyproof our house: padding such as bubble wrap around sharp corners of the coffee table, plastic shields for the electrical outlets, locks blocking access to low cabinets containing toxic cleaning products, and a baby gate at the basement stairs. Those precautions make sense for a toddler. But eventually, a kid benefits from a few bumps and bruises, both real and figurative, to learn how to get through tough times. Coping skills are like muscles—the more you use them, the stronger and more reliable they are.

As I started to grow older, the physical protections and barriers were replaced with more subtle, emotional protection. For one thing, my parents used my older brother's experiences to help shape mine. He had a wonderful fifth grade teacher, so my parents made sure I had the same one.[1] In high school, my brother had a rough experience with one of the math teachers, so my parents ensured I wouldn't be in her classroom. I played tennis as he did (but not nearly as well). In other words, I was fully bubble-wrapped! My brother paved the way—he made sure it was safe. There was no need for me to veer in a different direction.

The deleterious impact on my psyche was this: I would wonder, not infrequently, if my teachers really liked me for me and my own efforts, or if I got good grades because of my brother's success. Linked to this lack of confidence, I developed what I now understand as performance anxiety before and during my teen years—psyching myself out at crucial moments of a tennis match and losing the point; suddenly freezing during a piano recital, unable to finish on my own; and losing my train of thought during a classroom presentation, resulting in me stumbling over my words, my face turning scarlet, wishing to just be out of the spotlight.

My brother's experiences eclipsed mine, by no fault of his own. Like most smart kids growing up in a small town with limited possibilities, he was just trying to do well enough to move on to better things, preferably somewhere

---

1. Mr. M had actually kind of lost it by the time I got to fifth grade. He was quick to anger if not all the kids were keeping up. He would turn all red and scold us. He must have been going through some sort of personal crisis. All I know is he was not very inspirational or even stable when I had him as a teacher.

less provincial. It was my parents' choice (perhaps somewhat unconscious, even automatic) to venerate his position as the elder male child. Because he was a boy, my parents were less fearful for his safety.

Not surprisingly, he exercised a fair amount of independence as a teenager. He went out with friends and didn't even have a curfew that I can recall.

ANXIETY OVERLOAD

The metaphorical bubble wrap went beyond trying to shield me from educational upsets. My mother's anxiety over my safety permeated so many of my early experiences. At no more than age seven or eight, I was angry about something my brother had done. I marched up to my room, lined up all my stuffed animals, and said goodbye to each one. I then drew a picture and wrote a note saying I was running away from home. I stewed in my room for a while and then got over it. (I probably had a hankering for a fruit roll-up or cheesy popcorn.) I crumpled the picture and note, throwing them in my bedroom trash can, replaced my stuffed animals neatly on my bookshelf, and went downstairs to play with my dolls on the back porch, snack in hand. Later, almost time for dinner, I bounced down to the family room where my parents sat on the couch watching the evening news. My mom was shaking and wouldn't make eye contact with me. "Your mom is really upset," my dad said evenly, dispassionately. I saw the crumpled picture and note between them, spread open. I was mortified. But I had thrown it away! I didn't really mean that I wanted to run away.

My mom didn't speak to me or make eye contact with me for what seemed like an eternity, but it was probably only a day or so. She never sat down and spoke to me about it. The underlying message received by my young mind, whether intentional or not, was to not rebel or show anger. To unintentionally cause a parent intense emotional pain at such a young age was devastating.

Years later, when I got my driver's license at sixteen, I was excited and hopeful. I thought: "Finally, freedom!" Shortly after getting my license, a teammate on my tennis team, Crystal, invited me to hit the ball around one Saturday afternoon. We met at the high school courts. I was so happy I could drive there all by myself. We played for an hour and then went to McDonalds for a snack.

When I got home, my mother was up in arms. I wasn't home at the time she expected me. I was gone ninety minutes instead of sixty. She ran to me as I drove into the driveway and exclaimed, "I was sure you got into an accident! I drove around looking for you!" My mood, elevated thanks to exercise and much needed peer interaction, plummeted at my mother's panicked reaction. Later, sitting at the kitchen table over dinner, she elaborated calmly, trying to rationalize her oversized reaction, "I'm not worried about your driving—it's the others on the road."

I was so afraid of making my mother afraid.

There were still temptations, though, to try to carve out my own identity. Once in high school, around age seventeen, I tried my hand at a little rebellion. One weekday, I stayed after school (after notifying my parents) to play tennis with June, a classmate who used to be on the tennis team. I admired June. She laughed easily, had a unique style of dress that she often accessorized with anklets—unusual in our largely conventional small town—and had an overall positive energy to her. Plus, we had overprotective parents in common. Originally from India, her parents often questioned her about her whereabouts and decried her interest in romantic comedies (which they thought encouraged poor, Western morals), though this did not seem to deter her much.

After we hit the ball around, she introduced me to another friend, Kate, who was a bit younger than us. Kate seemed smart and well put together in a nonconventional, Molly Ringwald from *Sixteen Candles* sort of way. I learned that Kate had a boyfriend in a town about forty-five minutes away, and she was dying to see him. They talked about going to the boyfriend's house on Saturday night, but were still figuring out transportation. It was fun chatting with them, but I knew I had to get home. I jumped in the 1976 Oldsmobile inherited from my mother's parents a few years back. It was as large as a boat, but it functioned fine to get back and forth to school, and offered a small taste of independence.

June knew I had access to a car. She called me at the end of that week, a Saturday morning, and asked me to drive Kate and her to the boyfriend's house—they had no car, and they thought I'd have fun hanging out. June, obviously experienced at parent manipulation, walked me through a story to convince my parents.

"OK," I responded. "Let's do it!" I so wanted to have an adventure and meet new people. We would be the stars in our own John Hughes film: Kate, June, and me, three adventurous small-town teens asserting our independence and making memories, thanks to me and my Oldsmobile—a sweet ride!

As nonchalantly as possible, I approached my mom later that morning. "Hey Mom. Can I use the car tonight to go over to June's house? We're going to study a little and hang out."

Sounds like a predictable plotline of your run-of-the-mill sitcom, doesn't it? Lying to hang out with friends is something most teenagers do as easily as breathing. But as I spoke, butterflies filled my stomach, and my hands trembled behind my back. My mom was suspicious. Not only was my demeanor odd, I never went anywhere at night on my own. She got my brother involved; he happened to be home from college for a long weekend. He'd barely begun questioning me before I caved. "Actually, it's no big deal. Um…Changing my mind. I don't need the car tonight after all. I'm staying in."

I retreated to the empty den off the family room and called June to break my promise. Her disappointment was palpable, but I'd made my choice. My feelings could only be described as a weird, contradictory mix of regret and relief. Not surprisingly, I didn't see much of June and Kate after that, except for an occasional, casual hello in the high school hallways.

COULD WE ALL JUST TAKE A CHILL PILL?

Adding to the stress in the household were my father's and brother's quick tempers. They weren't physically aggressive, but were prone to swearing and yelling when frustrated, often at inanimate objects. My dad would drop a dish after dinner and swear, "This goddamn plate!" Driving in traffic with my dad invariably involved very colorful language. A common utterance: "Cocksucker!" Or, sometimes more instructively: "Use your goddamn signal next time. It's the little stick on the left!" And this was in relatively tame, small-town "traffic."

All of our daily routines were punctuated regularly by the male household members' varying degrees of verbal outrage.[2] My dad and brother bickered a lot with each other, sometimes over me crying in reaction to my brother's teasing. Their verbal explosions were difficult to be around and surely added to my mother's anxiety. She was a peacekeeper, wanting everyone to get along, as did I. I studied hard and got good grades, doing my best to not make any waves.

But, inevitably, I was an annoying little sister to my brother. We had plenty of everyday sibling rivalry. I remember talking a lot to my cat, Princess, in a high baby voice, which drove him nuts. We fought over the TV remote and who got the last bowl of popcorn. He popped the heads off my Barbie dolls when I wasn't around. Typical stuff.

In middle school, when I did have a few friends, my brother gave them juvenile, derogatory nicknames, which, again, is not surprising for a teenage boy. But my dad laughed at these jokes about my friends, implicitly condoning this behavior. Though possessing a stellar intellect, my dad typically lacked the emotional intelligence necessary to promote confidence and a sense of self-worth in a preteen girl. My mom might have said a thing or two about this in protest, trying to protect me, but overall it was a male-dominated household. Her efforts to smooth things over for me, unfortunately, never had a seismic effect on the family dynamics.

GHOSTS OF THE PAST

In retrospect, it makes sense that my dad would be ignorant to the sensitive nature of preteen girls. He'd been an only

---

2. We even had a family dog, taken in as a stray, who was pretty temperamental. He bit everyone in the family, except for my dad, at least once.

child, lived through the Great Depression, and served in World War II. He rarely spoke of his own father but, when he did, it seemed his own dad was rough around the edges. My paternal grandfather, who died before I was born, was injured working on the railways before the Great Depression and could no longer work to support his family, leaving him grumpy and emotionally distant.

To be fair, my own father showed affection other ways—buying me books on topics I expressed an interest in (from Van Gogh to Rasputin), fixing me popcorn after school, making the whole family elaborate Sunday breakfasts, teaching me with surprising patience[3] to drive a stick shift, and on and on.

My mother, too, had a rough-around-the-edges dad. She was the oldest of three and had to do a lot of grunt work on the family farm. She was raised in a small, two-bedroom home in rural Nebraska[4] right by the train tracks. When her youngest sibling was born, the only boy, my mom and her sister were removed from their shared bedroom and made to sleep in the living room. The family's only son apparently needed his own room. That dynamic alone probably taught her something about the importance of boys in comparison to girls and, years later, surreptitiously informed her parenting style. One of my childhood development classes referred to this as "ghosts in the nursery," based on a study showing that major life experiences—often traumatic—are passed down from generation to generation in some way or another.[5]

---

3. Yes! He abstained from swearing while teaching me to drive!
4. Rural Nebraska—is that redundant? No, I guess there's Omaha.
5. If interested, see: Fraiberg, Selma, Edna Adelson, and Vivian Shapiro. "Ghosts in the Nursery: A Psychoanalytic Approach to the Problems of Impaired Infant-Mother Relationships." *Journal of the American Academy of Child Psychiatry* 14, No. 3 (1975): 387–421.

WITHDRAWING—THE PATH OF LEAST RESISTANCE

By the time I got to high school, between my mom's fears about my safety and my insecurity in finding friends who would meet my family's approval, I found it easier to withdraw socially than try to navigate social circles. It was safer to be on my own. Summers were very lonely for me because I lacked the reliable structure of the school day. I was typically on my own in the summer, reading a lot and playing tennis on the odd occasion.[6]

Secretly, I held out for college. Right after my sophomore year in high school, I sat alone in my room, the long, empty summer months looming before me. Surrounded by a myriad of books that kept me company (mostly classics like Harper Lee's *To Kill a Mockingbird,* Richard Wright's *Native Son,* Aldous Huxley's *Brave New World,* and Charlotte Bronte's *Jane Eyre,* to name a few of my favorites), I thought, "Things will be different in college. I'll make friends and finally get a life."

I was accepted to the University of Illinois in Urbana-Champaign, the same college as my brother. I hesitated to take the same path as he, but I applied for and was offered a full-ride veteran's scholarship based on my father's military service, which was impossible to turn down. My mother was visibly relieved when I made the decision to go to the same college, where she thought he would protect me—the never-ending roll of bubble wrap! (Though she clung to this idea that my brother would guide me, he actually didn't

---

6. My parents, in contrast, were quite social. My mother hosted dinner parties and belonged to a few organizations independent from my father, including a drama club. This dichotomy between my own social isolation in comparison to the rest of my family's seemingly healthy social opportunities still tends to boggle my mind to this day, no matter how many theories I posit to explain it neatly away.

want much to do with me during that one year we overlapped at university. Understandably, he had his own life.)

Finally, in early August of my eighteenth year, as I was packing for college, my mother slinked into my room and said sadly, "I wish I could go with you." I was speechless. I wasn't equipped to help her at this juncture.

As eager as I was to move out, I didn't realize social skills grow from "normal" high school experiences and friendships. I really didn't have much of that due to the metaphorical padding around me all through my adolescence. I probably headed into college with the social skills of a twelve-year-old. I was book smart, but not street smart. I can't blame peers for avoiding me, in high school or college. I wanted to please and was nice, but was quite immature. Not too relatable.

Whew, that was rough. But I've cracked the nutshell of my first eighteen years in as few words as possible—enough to understand some context for my entrance into adulthood without becoming mired in tedious detail. Time to see what life after age eighteen had in store for me.

CHAPTER 2

From Voltaire to Au Pair

My initial college experiences can best be described as a fish out of water. I was assigned to a triple-capacity dorm room in a women's dormitory near the Quad, conveniently located relatively close to many of my classes. The first roommate I met on move-in day was Shelly, a party girl from St. Charles, Illinois, a suburb of Chicago. She proudly pointed to her big hair (which I honestly didn't notice) that first day and chirped, "I know, it's big. I'm known for my big hair."

Our other roommate, Megan, was a sullen, goth-type character from Deerfield, another Chicago suburb. She was also a self-proclaimed nymphomaniac. Luckily, most of her amorous adventures took place in her partners' dorm rooms, not ours. Megan also had never done laundry a day in her life, and she wasn't about to start once she was in college. She bought new underwear once in a while, and her clothes just piled up in a corner by her bed.[7] Another fun fact about Megan: One of her classes conflicted with

---

7. Eventually, her close friend, Sophia, an equally eccentric dorm dweller originally from Romania, did Megan's laundry periodically, saving us money in air freshener.

the broadcast time of *Yo! MTV Raps,* and nine times out of ten she skipped class to watch her favorite show. She had her priorities.

I wanted to fit in and be liked, but my freshman-year roommates and I just didn't jell. On occasion, I went out with Shelly and her friends to frat parties, but I didn't feel like I fit in, with or without alcohol as a social lubricant. Drinking alcohol (usually cheap beer from kegs) didn't erase my naivety—it just made it easier to flirt with guys and let my hair down. But when I sobered up the next morning, I was the same shy, awkward young woman as before.

Aside from tagging along with Shelly and her party-going friends on weekends, I managed to have friendly lunches in the downstairs cafeteria with a few more moderate residents in my college dorm. But I didn't become close friends with anyone in particular. I mostly buried myself in my studies—a familiar coping technique from high school to avoid awkward social situations.

In my sophomore year, I stayed in the dorm but moved to a double with a more middle-of-the-road roommate. I tried getting out more after befriending Crystal, an acquaintance from my hometown (who I had occasionally played tennis with). She was a year younger than me and happened to reside in the same dorm, a couple of floors down. She was outgoing and had a lot of friends going into college.

Turns out we shared a similar goofy sense of humor and love of late-night Scrabble games, and became good friends. We explored the campus bars and after parties, but I ended up in one too many misadventures in the underage bar scene. Predictably, my hangovers were too often accompanied by cringeworthy flashes of my drunken make-out sessions with random guys. Not a great fit for me either.

My junior year, at age twenty, I decided to find greater independence and expand my world by embarking on a big adventure: a yearlong study abroad program in Paris.

DEPARTURE AND ARRIVAL

It was my first time living so far from home on my own. Living across the Atlantic was a big deal. When I moved just an hour's drive away to attend university at eighteen, my mother had been, predictably, ambivalent. She managed her empty-nester dis-ease by visiting me weekly for Sunday brunch, my dad happily in tow. Her daughter moving seven hours away by plane to study at the Sorbonne put her in a tailspin, though she was outwardly supportive. (Remember, this is before smartphones and videoconferencing.) In contrast, I was excited and hopeful this adventure would lead to amazing adventures, independence, and a path forward that my parents—and I—could be proud of.

Still, a palpable, overwhelming surge of anxiety hit me right before boarding the plane. "Wait a minute," I thought, "What the hell… I know absolutely no one else in this program. I'm severing ties to all that's familiar. What have I done?"

I suspect my mom's anxiety had implanted itself in my psyche and rose to the surface at this point of no return. (She was so nervous at the airport and told me to call home right when I landed.) Fortunately, during the plane ride, I sat next to another program enrollee, Darlene. Her cheerful, chatty personality dissolved the rocks in the pit of my stomach. It also didn't hurt that Air France offered a French-inspired dinner, complete with a complimentary glass of wine.

A junior year abroad in Paris made sense academically: my major was French literature with a minor in history. I'd studied French throughout high school. French opened doors to a new world, helping me transcend my small-town existence. Many of my co-travelers, also enrolled in university, were majoring in French business. I must have believed I would be able to support myself one day on my intellectual prowess and highfalutin panoramic knowledge of French literature and culture. I held nothing against my co-travelers on the French business track. In fact, I stayed friends with several of them for many years. Why they accepted me readily into their friend groups despite my many naïve and clueless ways, however, remains somewhat a mystery. But I was thankful.

Once in France, we had two weeks in a dorm before we had to find housing on our own. There were two tracks. Either we paid ("we" meaning "our parents") for an apartment in Paris, or we found an au pair position where a French family provided housing, and typically a stipend, in exchange for childcare and often light house keeping. All positions allowed us to attend classes at the Sorbonne during the day, earning college credits that would transfer to our respective universities.

The other au-pair-bound students and I were somewhat frantic about this two-week deadline. Using French in the classroom—a sympathetic audience—to prattle on about the role of the Voltaire during the Enlightenment[8] or Camus's existentialism[9] was one thing. Negotiating with

---

8. Voltaire is well known for *Candide*, which I studied in high school, in a college history class, and in my college French lit class. A very funny read, *Candide* also offers many philosophical gems.
9. Existentialism is a fascinating philosophy, but Camus's novels are compelling in their own right, such as *The Fall*. To paraphrase one of my favorite comedians and podcasters, Tig Notaro, "I love a good twist and turn!"

French housewives about childcare arrangements to secure a roof over my head in a foreign city was entirely another. We were directed to ads listed by au pair agencies that acted as an intermediary between families and au pairs, as well as ads posted in the American church, which were not necessarily as well regulated.

Nervously, I practiced my spiel and, prepaid phonecard in hand, went to a nearby payphone to begin responding to au pair ads. (Things were rough in the early '90s.)

On my first call, a woman answered the phone in English with an Irish brogue. She asked if I had experience with childcare and housework. Relaxing slightly and abandoning my well-practiced French, I said, "Yes, I have experience babysitting and am available in the afternoons after class."

She explained the job included ironing the family's clothes and asked if I'd be willing to comply. I paused and stammered. (Typically, I wore pretty basic clothes that didn't need ironing: bulky sweaters, blue jeans, oversized T-shirts.) Before I could answer with a polite, "Yes, I'll do anything. I'm a hard worker," she jumped in with, "Of course not, you Americans never want to work for anything."

I was taken aback. I thought, "Why did she hate Americans?" Perhaps more importantly, I should have asked myself, "Why can't she iron her own clothes?"

Rattled, I mumbled, "Thanks for your time," and hung up.

I tried another phone number from an au pair ad posted in the American church, not through a typical au pair agency. This initial exchange over the phone was courteous and promising. Feeling hopeful, I agreed to meet with Madame Didier, who lived in a posh residential area near the Bois de Boulogne, where Roland Garros hosts the French Open every year. I brought along my new friend Darlene.

A quick aside about Darlene—I can't remember if she was also a French business major, or maybe just minoring in French. I do remember that while very sweet and friendly (which I needed), she was also perhaps even more naïve than I, which is hard to believe, because I was pretty green.

She seemed homesick from day three, after the jet lag started to wear off. For example, she complained about any barely noticeable dirt in the spiral staircases of the dorms and apartment buildings we toured. She'd brag, "My mom cleans everything," followed by a lament such as, "This city seems so dirty!"

She was also tempted to accept a ride from a man at the train station when we first arrived. Mind you, I had pretty much zero worldly experience. If you measured street smarts the way you measured alcohol content, I was at best a light beer. Still, I somehow knew that strange men trolling the train station for *les jeunes filles américaines* weren't good news.

Darlene graciously accompanied me on the Métro ride to this near-Paris suburb. The walk to the house was an additional fifteen minutes from the train stop. We came to the residential neighborhood of the Didier family, consisting of rows of townhomes, all gated, close together, and tall. I'd rehearsed interview answers beforehand in my best French. I knew my syntax wasn't perfect. Prepositions are difficult in any language, and I'm sure I didn't know all the idioms that would have made me sound more fluent.

Despite my nerves during the interview, when one of the kids came up to the mother with a detached button in hand, I offered to sew it back on for her. Why did I have my travel sewing kit with me? I have no idea. I can count on one hand the number of times I've ever sewn a button back onto a piece of clothing. But, eager to please, I did a quick sewing job in front of Madame Didier. She was delighted. A regular Mary Poppins in her midst! She offered me the job caring for the two younger girls—Colette and Pauline, 6 and 8, respectively.

Darlene, my sweet but misguided friend, loved that my lodging would be in the family's house. Riding back to the dorm on the Métro, she couldn't stop singing the praises of this arrangement and envied my position. "You'll be part of the family," she crooned.

I actually felt a little nervous about being so close under the same roof with strangers.

A more common arrangement for most au pairs in Paris is to be housed independently in the "servant's quarters," units in the top floor of most apartment buildings, with the family living in the rooms below. A unit typically includes a small furnished room with a sink, a hot plate, and an entirely separate entrance from the family's living space. The bathroom is shared by all residents on the floor, usually with Turkish toilets—where you place one foot on each side of the toilet hole and squat over it. (Other residents on the old servant's floor may be other au pairs of families in the building and immigrant families.) Au pairs commonly have shower privileges in the family's bathroom as prearranged. Initially, this type of arrangement appealed to me more because it seemed to offer more independence during off-work hours.

Taking a cue from my friend's sparkling enthusiasm and dismissing my own slight trepidation, I took the job. I reasoned that I needed a place to stay and time was ticking. It seemed the safe choice. (I didn't realize it at the time, but this was one of many decisions born of my aversion to risk, a recurring tension between seeking adventure and needing safety.) I convinced myself: Living with a family this close could be culturally enriching and so great for my French. In exchange for less independence from the family, my language skills would grow in such an immersive environment. Or so I thought.

DOMESTIC DETOUR

I was to meet the girls at school on certain days to walk them home, fix them a snack, make a light dinner, draw their baths, and see them to bed. I also had to iron their clothes (but not the adults' or teenagers' clothes). My bedroom was on the top floor of the house with my own bathroom, equipped with a hot plate, small fridge, a few dishes, and a plastic bin in which to wash dishes; the top floor had two more bedrooms, for their sixteen-year-old daughter, Eveline, and fourteen-year-old son, Luc, who'd use the second-floor bathroom. No stipend or food was included—just lodging.

My upstairs bedroom was comfortable enough—it had a cheap but functional loveseat, coffee table, small writing desk, and a night stand. The bed was under a drop ceiling, so I couldn't sit up in bed and would literally have to roll out of bed in the morning. The mattress on my bed had a severe indentation. I slept smack dab in the middle of the mattress, which sank three to four inches lower than either side. Obviously, it was a hand-me-down. I pondered the first night, "How old is this thing? And how may au pairs have slept here before?" But I was only twenty and not one to complain. I was in Paris to explore the city—I didn't expect luxury accommodations.

The rest of the house was a taxidermist's dream. Monsieur Didier apparently liked to hunt or at least to acquire hunting-themed artifacts. The foyer contained no fewer than four taxidermized items: a badger umbrella stand (claws drawn, teeth flashing, as if ready to attack), deer antlers above the entrance to the living room, a wall-mounted bird of some sort, and a bearskin rug leading to the dining area. Other delightful items I would discover during my stay included a rabbit-fur-lined nutcracker in the kitchen drawer and moose antlers mounted in Monsieur Didier's downstairs den. The carpet was blood red—nice touch. I was vegetarian. Perhaps a house full of taxidermy tchotchkes was not the ideal place to call home for nine months. Again, though I noticed the unusual décor during the interview, I suppressed any hesitation in favor of immediate security—a roof over my head was paramount, taxidermy be damned.

As for the childcare responsibilities that awaited me, I had no concerns. I had always gotten along with children and anticipated no problems with childcare. At age fifteen, I babysat for a neighborhood family with twin boys, a younger daughter, and an older, nonverbal daughter with significant physical and mental disabilities. She sat on the floor and rocked, and wore mittens to prevent her from biting her hands. She was actually a little older than me. When alone with her—sometimes they needed a sitter just for her—my instinct was to speak with her in a normal, friendly tone about my day, what was going on with the family, or the TV show I was watching. I felt for her. Who knows, I'd thought, maybe she understands a little bit and enjoys my voice.

Another family I sat for more regularly was also wonderful: The baby was one or two when I started caring for her; her older siblings were around six and eight. I made simple meals for them on the stove—hot dogs, mac and cheese, scrambled eggs. We played with toys, read books, played games, and watched TV. Everyone got along. I liked it. It was a peaceful household.

Colette and Pauline were different. Colette, the youngest, had a cute, cherub face and could be loving away from her sister, but was susceptible to her sister's influences when they were together. Pauline was mean. She constantly ridiculed my accent and grammar and would point out immediately if I made a gender mistake. I might accidentally say, "Le bain est chaude" (adding feminine to the adjective inappropriately), or "sois gentil" (leaving off the feminine pronunciation for the adjective)—that sort of thing.

Pauline had a lazy eye, technically called amblyopia. I later learned that she seemed to have some sort of learning disability, though I wasn't sure if the eye condition was related. She was taken periodically to an eye specialist and also had a tutor after school a few days a week. She struggled.

My presence as an inferior American served to make her miserable life a little cheerier. Maybe she struggled in school, but at least she could speak French and keep her pronouns and articles straight, unlike that poor, dumb American girl. I'm using "poor" in the financial sense—she took absolutely no pity on me. She once told me that I was only an au pair because I didn't have money to live elsewhere. Obviously, this came from her parents, and from their aristocratic view on the world. Wanting to improve my French and immerse myself in the culture did not enter their minds as possible reasons I wanted to be an au pair. The older children, Eveline and Luc, were seen mainly in passing, and I had a neutral rapport with them, at best polite and detached.

I cannot overstate the extent of my naïve, deferential nature at this young age. An immature twenty-year-old, I was terribly shy, trusting, and not equipped to assert myself.

A more assertive, confident au pair would have probably managed better in that environment. But I was embarrassed by my syntax errors and would hesitate to practice my French in front of them. I didn't have the confidence to argue in French, even with schoolchildren.

Aside from the children's taunts, myriad other aspects squashed any illusion of a cozy, familial atmosphere. I was secluded in my upstairs bedroom when not caring for the children. I was never invited to casual family meals or other activities where I could interact with the adults. This family considered au pairs as lower-class workers. Interacting with au pairs outside of childcare duties would have offended their sensibilities. This wasn't the experience of all au pairs. Ellen, Winnie, and a few other students who were also au pairs sometimes had Sunday dinner with the families or went on excursions in the city together.

I learned how little childcare was valued in this family, and likely within much of the au pair culture as a whole. Madame Didier never corrected her children when they were making fun of me. Typically, she was around, in the other room reading a magazine or chatting on the phone. Apparently, she ran a business selling children's clothes, but I never witnessed her actually working. Her detached air puzzled me. (Her husband was a lawyer and rarely around, except later in the evening.) Why would you want the person in charge of your children to feel denigrated? But the kids had a new au pair every year. Better to ridicule them and test the boundaries than to get too attached, I theorized.

Apparently, the family was equally dissatisfied with me. I could imagine Madame gossiping with her friends, "She can barely boil an egg or iron a pair of girls' pants." Huh, maybe the angry Irish lady was onto something after all. But then again, I was not intentionally underperforming at domestic chores. When told to use more force with ironing, I adjusted my technique. When told to set a two-minute timer for the perfect egg, I complied. Maybe it was too little, too late.

In early March, my stress over this living arrangement reached a new level. I reached a tipping point after glancing in Monsieur Didier's basement office, near the TV room where I ironed clothes and Luc, the only boy in the house, tried to sneak in to watch "Dukes of Hazzard" dubbed in French.[10] Imagine my surprise when I saw multiple posters of Monsieur Didier campaigning for a local political position under the Jean-Marie Le Pen's National Front. According to my limited knowledge of the French political landscape, Le Pen supporters, known for their anti-immigration, nationalist platform, seemed to hate foreigners. I was a foreigner. Their Polish house cleaner was a foreigner. "Why did they even hire us?" I wondered.

I was no longer just aggravated by the mean little girls and the menial, thankless tasks; I was afraid of their political stance. They hated me not only for being an au pair without means, but for being an American. Yes, this sounds melodramatic now, but it accurately conveys my panicked headspace at the time.

Armed with this additional tidbit, my unexpressed resentment in reaction to the daily microaggressions grew unbearable.

SPRING INTO ACTION

In March, my friends called me at the house to invite me out for St. Patrick's Day. Madame Didier said I wasn't home

---

[10]. The French dubbing did nothing to improve the plot line of that show, but then again, I was never a fan.

(though I was). I was livid when I learned from them the next day that they'd tried to reach me. I did go out with my friends sometime after that when the family was out of town for the weekend. As I returned to the house, slightly tipsy, I entered the empty foyer. After carefully disarming then rearming the security alarm (which terrified me, since I'd set it off more than once in the past), I spit on the badger umbrella stand.

He responded as usual, stretched vertically and balanced firmly on his hindquarters, eternally flashing his fangs and extending his sharp talons, forever ready to strike. "Poor creature," I thought. "I shouldn't take it out on you. You probably died defending your turf." I paused and softened a bit more: "Now look at you—just an umbrella receptacle in this house of horrors." Bidding the umbrella stand good night, I cut the lights and climbed carefully up the steep stairs to my bedroom, to sink into my well-worn mattress and dream of better days.

As the mild, sunny springtime weather began to permeate the Parisian boulevards, streets, and alleyways, the sidewalk cafés filled with happy patrons. The parks bloomed and people picnicked. I, however, was miserable. Springtime in Paris, I thought, should not be experienced through this toxic lens. After calling my parents for an advance in funds, I found an apartment to rent for the rest of my stay totaling about eight weeks.

When I tearfully announced my plans to leave, Madame Didier snapped back at me with an accusatory retort. Apparently, as she explained it, she had once entered my bathroom with a repairman and found it to be quite dirty. She quipped, "J'avais honte," translated as, "I was ashamed."

Looking back, I'm sure I cleaned my bathroom/kitchen combo occasionally, but not daily. I had a bathtub, but no shower, so the tub probably got kind of dirty. And I mainly cooked spaghetti and sauce on my hot plates for dinner, so I imagine there was some red splatter here and there. I had to wash dishes in the same sink in which I brushed my teeth. I did my best at the time to creatively juggle my self-care and culinary supplies in that close space.

By the way, let's not forget I was living in *Paris*—home of the Eiffel Tower, Orsay Museum, Notre Dame, Champs-Elysées, Pompidou Center, and bakeries galore. I prioritized exploring the city and keeping up with schoolwork over deep cleaning.

AMERICANS IN PARIS

From day one, despite struggling with my living situation, I was hungry to soak up as much French culture as possible. I took advantage of the field trips the program arranged, including weekend excursions to amazing sites such as Chartres Cathedral, Mont Saint-Michel, and Versailles.

I explored other sites on my own or with other students in the program. I loved the Rodin Museum, off the beaten path in a more residential neighborhood, with its serene outdoor exhibits and intimate indoor galleries. I favored the Orsay Museum over the Louvre, the former housing more later-period works that captivated me. And as for the French bakeries (pâtisseries), all I can say is, "Oui, oui!" Chocolate croissants, fruit tartlets, fresh baguettes… it was heaven.

Equally enjoyable was the café culture. Sitting at a sidewalk café in the Latin Quarter gazing at the Seine, with either a friend or a book for company, felt like a true Parisian experience.

I hung out with Winnie and Ellen most often. They became fast friends after sitting next to each other on the plane from Chicago, and I managed to insert myself into their sphere once our classes started at the Sorbonne, hanging out with them before and after classes. Ellen was majoring in French business at the University of Illinois at Chicago, while Winnie was pursuing the same major at the Urbana-Champaign campus.

We enjoyed perusing the Latin Quarter, including sitting by the Seine with a bottle of wine on the occasional evening. It was one of those nights that my inner "Cousin It," inspired by the Addams Family character by the same name, revealed itself. I had longer hair and glasses, and would throw my hair forward over my face and place my glasses on over my hair. Winnie and Ellen have many photos of Cousin It in Paris playing the tourist; in one he is gazing at Notre Dame. In another, he is frolicking in the Luxembourg Gardens. He even poses pensively next to Rodin's *The Thinker*.

I managed to travel outside of Paris from time to time with my newfound American pals. Winnie and I took a memorable day trip to Auvers-sur-Oise in late fall to visit the famous church painted by Van Gogh, behind which is his grave site. We toured the nearby museum in Doctor Gachet's old house, where Van Gogh lived for a short time recovering from a mental breakdown. It was a privilege to explore the same grounds frequented by my favorite artist.

Later in the academic year, several of us—Winnie, Ellen, Darlene, a few other classmates, and I—visited Albertville, just as the 1992 Winter Olympics were winding down. We couldn't afford to attend any Olympic events but enjoyed wandering through the little town. It was unseasonably warm; the beautiful mountainous landscape incredibly calming. We all loved playing the tourist.

The classes at the Sorbonne were for the most part very engaging. They included art history, modern French poetry, film, Enlightenment literature, and French politics. We were in classes with other international students, so the professors were forgiving of our imperfect grammar.

In sum, I kept very busy outside of my au pair responsibilities, but these outside pursuits did not compensate for the coldness, bordering on hostility, in the Didier home.

AU REVOIR MADAME

Madame Didier was clearly indifferent to my life outside of being her children's au pair. Late March, when I announced I was moving out within the week, she took this final opportunity to express how inadequate my efforts were, that she was ashamed of my inadequate cleaning skills.

To move to my new apartment, I summoned Ellen and Winnie's help.

Winnie and Ellen were definitely more together than I was. Returning to the street smarts to alcohol content analogy, Winnie was a crisp, cool hard cider—off the beaten path. She was kind, funny, a bit quirky, and definitely goal-oriented. She had several younger siblings and was the first to go to college, which she took seriously.

Ellen was at least a bold merlot—she had been to Paris before and knew how to get around already. Rock star status. She was also the oldest sibling, the first to attend college, and from the big city of Chicago, so a bit tougher than those of us from the smaller midwestern towns. They had both found lasting au pair situations that included a small stipend, independent living quarters, and reasonable expectations.

Moving day was several days after my twenty-first birthday but fell smack dab on Ellen's birthday. She was a trouper. They both were. They helped me drag my bags on the Métro, including at least one train change, down the street of a different neighborhood to a rental with my own entrance (sans shrieking security alarm), private bath, and shared kitchen. They gave me the best birthday gift—a happy ending, finally, to my junior year abroad. I also came to appreciate the kindness and hospitality my parents demonstrated to any and all guests, acquaintances and strangers alike. Their values contrasted starkly with the Didiers'.

Circling back to the booze metaphor, I believe I progressed from light beer status to the craft beer realm of street smarts. As rocky as that move was, my literal baggage was much easier to manage than my emotional kind. Turns out, I had a long way yet to go with the emotional baggage in tow.

CHAPTER 3

The French Disconnection

EXISTENTIAL EXIT

A year later, I graduated with my French bachelor of arts and a minor in history. Majoring in the humanities offers rich insights into history, psychology, and the arts but seldom leads straight to a related career. Lacking common sense at this age, I had no forethought on how I'd make a living.

After the pomp and circumstance of graduation and a celebratory dinner with my extended family, existential dread engulfed me. Sartre and Camus weren't going to be much help during this crisis, unless they could reincarnate themselves and stop by with some groceries and rent money.

Besides the practical paycheck issue, I felt shiftless. "Without the structure of college classes," I agonized, "what will I do with myself?" I felt like I was waiting for Godot, where Godot represented a gig where I could get paid for lounging around coffee shops, reading literature, and munching on pastries. I was good at being a student—I knew that from both high school and college. What else was I good at?

Amid my angst, I recalled the powerful, no-nonsense words of Marian Wright Edelman, the commencement speaker at my alma mater and an accomplished civil rights and children's advocate. She urged my graduating class to waste no time in tackling the inequities in society, to use our knowledge and skills for the greater good.

That summer, inspired by Edelman's message, I signed up to volunteer at a local domestic violence shelter, starting by helping on the administrative side. Then I took a forty-hour domestic violence training, allowing me to help run children's groups and answer their hotline, while I scraped by financially via a bookkeeping job at a homeowner's association. I was even nominated Volunteer of the Year by the shelter's volunteer coordinator. My passion for the place was intense.

Likening it to a domestic Peace Corps experience, I found that helping others in dire circumstances sparked a powerful, motivating force in me. Despite these strong feelings, I never thought of transitioning into a social services-related career. I held to the narrative that I had to do something more academic or intellectual to earn a living, following in my dad's footsteps as well as those of my brother, who was already earning a master's degree in his field.

FRANCE: VERSION 2.0

After my post-college gap year volunteering at the shelter, I stuck with French and earned a master of arts in French literature. During this period, I lived alone in a studio apartment near the university campus. I was awarded a tuition waiver by the French Department, but to pay for rent and other living expenses, I worked the night shift at the domestic violence shelter two to three nights a week. It paid relatively well. I answered the crisis line and helped the women staying in the shelter manage the nightly chores. It was an odd dichotomy: French literature by day, crisis management by night.

My two-year experience getting an MA in French lit was rich fodder for my nerdy, literature-loving self. I got a kick out of almost all of my classes, from medieval French to modern, post-colonial literature. But I remained socially stagnant. The program consisted mostly of women already married or attached, so my social circle was limited. Ultimately, my continued studies in French helped me escape the question, "What do you want to do with your life?"

Upon earning my master's degree, at age twenty-five, I landed a one-year position teaching English in Dijon, France, at the University of Burgundy—a program offered through my alma mater's French Department.

The living situation in Dijon was far superior to that of Paris—I rented a small apartment from a lovely couple who occasionally brought me snacks or invited me up for a chat. My colleagues, also yearlong adjuncts in Dijon, came from England, New Zealand, and the US. I enjoyed my independence in Dijon and many parts of the job.

I hung out with these colleagues on various occasions. One memorable excursion was the Saint-Vincent Tournante wine festival (held that year in Les Maranges, within driving distance from Dijon) during which we were given wine glasses to wear around our necks as we walked from village to village, sampling the various wines of Burgundy. It was by far the best necklace I've ever worn!

In Dijon, I also discovered kir, a mixture of cassis and white wine, which originated in the region. It was fun getting to know the city's rich history and unique architecture (characterized by decorative rooftops). I traveled a bit around France during breaks; I went to Brittany on my own during one break but mostly explored the region right around Dijon.

Still, living abroad can be a lonely venture. I practiced my French with some students whose English was better than my French. We occasionally went to movies or cafés together, but my social life definitely didn't pop with constant activity, and dating was way off my radar. Though I was going on twenty-six, I was inexperienced and shy. I completely lacked motivation to try dating. Flashes of my lack of sophistication surely surfaced at times during interactions with my coworkers and French acquaintances.

I had no concrete plans for my return to the US except a vague notion that I could teach French in a community college or small liberal arts college. I stuck to that narrative with no real knowledge of the job market. I also hoped another year abroad would give me the worldly experience I still lacked, and my social deficits would be magically fixed.

BACK TO REALITY

To my dismay, after returning to the US, my intellectual prowess and immersion in French language and culture didn't immediately attract job offers left and right. I looked at job ads in local community colleges but was stumped.

I stayed with my parents while I tried to sort out my next move. I was pretty lost. My mother, a nurse, dropped major hints about me getting certified to teach high school French. This fell on deaf ears. High school was not, shall we say, the best time of my life. Though I had some amazing teachers who kept me excited about learning and hopeful about the future, I couldn't imagine voluntarily *going back* to high school, even in an adult teaching role. (She was also very vocal about me never becoming a nurse. She felt like it was often an oppressive position to be in, that she was at the mercy of doctors' egos. For that reason, I never had an interest in nursing or anything else in health care.)

My dad thought I could contact a headhunter to get a college teaching position. Apparently, this worked for him ages ago when he was searching for a high school teaching job in music, before he pursued his PhD. I didn't have to check the yellow pages for this one. A job placement agency for people with advanced degrees in French literature? I thought, "Um, sorry, Dad. Not a thing."

I wasn't confident enough in my French to go for a PhD. Though I was a good student, a PhD program requires confidence and initiative. Staying in academia ultimately intimidated me, even though it would have pleased my father.

However, French literature is clearly not a marketable discipline outside of academia or teaching. A business degree or teaching certificate might have been a good fallback, come to think of it. Insert your favorite cliché here:

"Hindsight is 2020."

"Live and learn."

"Get your shit together."

Wait, that last one isn't a cliché. It was my inner voice.

Motivated by that oh-so-friendly inner voice, I looked for opportunities that provided both a paycheck and health insurance. What a high bar. The next attempt at supporting myself included working at a library association in my university town doing mundane office work.

After I got that job, I found my own apartment away from my parents. Though I could have saved money staying with them, my mother freaked out again after I was gone more than a couple of hours reading at a nearby Borders bookstore—she thought something had happened to me. (Again, this is before cell phones.) I couldn't live with them any longer—it felt too suffocating.

Next, a year after my return from Dijon, I secured a job as a court advocate at the domestic violence shelter where I had worked with great dedication after my undergrad years. The job entailed helping victims of domestic abuse obtain court orders of protection, including completing paperwork that documented the abuse and accompanying them to court for moral support.

Court advocacy was rewarding at first but predictably ended in compassion fatigue. Toward the end of my tenure (which lasted around fourteen months), I witnessed a woman's abusive partner, who'd put out cigarettes on her skin when they were together, woo her back during a court recess at her two-year order of protection hearing. My stomach turned at the prospect of her returning to that abuser—I really felt physically ill. Such a turn of events isn't uncommon. All staff members at the shelter had witnessed such flip-flopping to varying degrees. It's the cycle of violence. In retrospect, I was perhaps too empathetic, and overly invested emotionally, for a job like that. It inevitably ended in burnout.

NOT INVINCIBLE

It would be disingenuous at this point to completely omit any description of my own messy social life. While I was advocating for women and children in crisis, I was on shaky ground in my own personal life.

A few months after my return from Dijon, circa 1997, I began a relationship with Liam, an acquaintance I'd met abroad through a mutual friend, Darlene. Remember Darlene, the friend who encouraged me to take the job with the Didier family? She and Liam became friends during law school—they both attended a law program in Belgium. I first met Liam briefly when I visited Darlene in Belgium during Easter break.

Darlene was engaged to a Frenchman from La Madeleine, near the Belgian border. The timing was perfect: The wedding was scheduled for the tail end of my teaching contract in Dijon. I got to know Liam much better at Darlene's wedding in June, which was small but lovely. Liam was well read, well traveled, and funny.

After the big event in La Madeleine, Liam and I were on the same flight back to Chicago. I'd planned to book a hopper plane back to Urbana-Champaign, where my parents lived at the time. Liam, though, was planning to pick up his car from his parents' place near O'Hare Airport and to drive downstate himself—he would be living in Champaign, having secured work at a small law firm. He offered to give me a ride to my parents'. I accepted.

We started out as good friends. He was rebounding from a breakup—his stateside girlfriend had dumped him shortly before Darlene's wedding. He sulked about it for a while in those first few weeks, but I enjoyed his company nonetheless, hanging out with him at bookstores and coffee shops. After several months of friendship, we became quite an item. It had taken me over a quarter of a century to enter a romantic relationship, which made the relationship that much more intense for me; I fell for him head over heels.

But, after about a year of dating, when he accepted a new job as an attorney in Chicago, he cut off the relationship. When I said, "Don't leave me here," Liam scolded me as if I were a child. "I'm not staying here to be your play pal," he barked. "How selfish of you."

As he spoke to me, he seemed to get stronger and more confident, even bigger in size, while I shrank into myself, speechless. My words were misinterpreted. I think I just meant to say, "I'll miss you."

Privately, I fell into a deep despair, as one often does after a major breakup, especially at a young age. Publicly, I held it together by arriving to work early and staying late. Inexperienced and embarrassed, I didn't know how or where to seek help.

As previously suggested, navigating romantic relationships was yet another important area in which I felt completely inept. I was definitely interested in boys during college but was terrified of them as well. It was all new to me.

Funny story: My sophomore year of college, my parents gave me a copy of *Lady Chatterley's Lover* by D.H. Lawrence, I suppose in an effort to teach me about sex. "Your mother and I thought this would be helpful as you continue in college," my dad stammered and left it at that. I'm not Jewish, and I don't intend to offend anyone with cultural appropriation, but if any moment merits a huge "oy vey," it was that one. Reading an early twentieth century novel about forbidden love across social classes didn't help me overcome my social awkwardness around the opposite sex.

After a couple of weeks, before he moved to Chicago, Liam and I reconciled as friends. I was miserable not being able to talk to him. I told myself I still wanted him as a friend because he was a very cool person—charismatic and cultured. (Sprinkle in a dash of misogyny and playboy persona, and you have a fuller portrait.) It seemed a promising compromise at the time.

After Liam moved to Chicago, Urbana-Champaign felt like a ghost town, as I had few ties remaining there outside my parents. My friend Winnie lived in her hometown, a suburb south of Chicago, and had married her college boyfriend in 1996, weeks before I left for Dijon. During that year after Dijon, I occasionally drove to Chicagoland to visit Winnie. I'd also often pay a visit to Ellen, who lived with her parents just north of Chicago—not unusual given the cost of living—and worked in an architecture firm downtown. Crystal, my hometown connection who befriended me my sophomore year of college, still lived in Champaign, but she had recently become engaged. We didn't hang out much—and I felt like a third wheel when we did.

Everyone else, it seemed, was moving on, evolving either professionally or personally, except for me. After Liam left for Chicago, I felt little hope for any future in Urbana-Champaign. Chicago, for many reasons, seemed a logical destination for me as well.

AN ODE TO THE WINDY CITY

In high school, I traveled yearly to Chicago with the French club. It was about a three-hour drive from my hometown.

We'd visit the Art Institute of Chicago, its mighty bronze lions guarding the entrance. The goal was usually to visit the impressionists, but we were given free rein to visit any area of the museum.

I loved the Van Goghs, the room of miniatures, and Chagall's stained glass. I loved seeing the multitude of diverse people, the excited buzz of like-minded tourists, and immersing myself ever so briefly in the exhilarating and liberating anonymity of big city life.

We would typically stop by Water Tower Place to do some window shopping, or real shopping. Though comical now, I was drawn to the Gap store. A young, idealistic white girl from a mostly Caucasian, homogeneous small town, I was the perfect target for the Gap's ads promoting togetherness, diversity, and Peace on Earth. One year, we saw *Les Misérables* at the Auditorium Theater. I was on cloud nine. Again, the themes of social justice and love conquering all appealed to my altruistic young psyche.

Even eating at the Au Bon Pain (or similar-type restaurant) across the street from the Art Institute was an adventure. For an idealistic teen from a small central Illinois town, yearning to see the world, what is not to love about Chicago? It was a mecca of summer festivals, diverse cuisine, lakefront scenery, museums, employment opportunities, and hip social scenes.

CHICAGO (AND SUBURBS), HERE I COME

Dreaming of the hustle and bustle of the Big City, I left the court advocate job at age twenty-eight, at the end of the summer, about three months after Liam moved away. With barely enough money saved up for a deposit on an apartment just outside Chicago, I planned my escape. Normally not one to lie to my parents, I was desperate and needed them to not worry about me, as they were wont to do. I felt I needed to distance myself from my parents geographically again (one function of my adventures abroad), and that Chicago, about a three-hour drive away from them, would not only be a parental buffer but also have opportunities for me, both personal and professional.

I convinced them on a shaky premise, that I had an offer to teach French enrichment to kids through Harper College just outside Chicago. While I did have a job offer, I left out the part about it being temporary and finite—it was only a three-month enrichment program.

After the part-time French teaching job, I managed to make ends meet working short-term administrative jobs through Manpower, a temp company, in the near-Chicago suburbs. I was an administrative temp for a hospital system during the Y2K scare—the crisis that never happened.[11]

After a few months living in Chicagoland, I applied for and accepted a legitimate full-time position with benefits at a nonprofit. I was ecstatic! This organization coordinated yearlong international learning exchanges, matching foreign high school students to American host families and placing American teens in learning opportunities abroad. The nonprofit's mission seemed noble and in line with my values: bring high school students to the US from other countries, place them in American host families, and let the cultural learning begin. This is

---

11. I helped assemble the instructional binders in case of a power failure at midnight December 31, 1999. Though the New Year arrived without incident, I got a cool "Team Y2K" T-shirt out of it.

surely how we can achieve world peace—one family at a time. It was the opposite of a funny slogan I once read on an anti-war T-shirt or poster in college—"Join the Army; travel to exotic, distant lands; meet exciting, unusual people and kill them."

CHAPTER 4

Planes, Trains, and Couch Surfing

My job was to coordinate volunteers in select Wisconsin and Illinois communities. In turn, these volunteers recruited host families for incoming international students.

I was one of three new hires as part of a restructuring of the Midwestern office—Cindy and Drew assumed similar roles working with different communities. There had been some sort of brouhaha before we arrived. I don't know if other workers had been fired or moved elsewhere in the organization. Three other employees, in addition to the director, had worked there for at least a couple of years: Kim, a psychologist to help problem-solve student-family conflicts; Sonia, an office clerk; and Lily, a recruiter for American high school students considering studying abroad.

Cindy, Drew, and I were assigned to respective regions across Illinois, Missouri, and Wisconsin to work with volunteers living in those areas. Our duties consisted of sending profiles of students seeking placements, furnishing the volunteers with training materials and tips on cultural integration, and planning orientations for incoming students and their families.

The placement of students worked sort of like a dating service: Julianne from Sweden loves (insert hobbies) and has X siblings. Cannot live with a smoker but loves dogs. Or, commonly, a profile would state: casual smoker and is allergic to animals. The smokers were fun to place. Families also had their own profiles that the students received before moving in with the assigned family.

Our boss, Petra, was a German native with a fairly thick accent. She seemed very enthusiastic about my travel experience and hired me after one interview. She even invited me out for a glass of wine before my first day of work, which troubled me a bit. During that rendezvous, she made vague statements about loyalty and respect, or something to that effect. I didn't understand it and it made me uncomfortable, but I really wanted a job with a real salary and not just hourly temp work. I repressed the icky feeling and tried to focus on the positive—I had a new full-time job with benefits and a noble mission. Plus, I was dazzled by "international" in the name of the organization.

After a brief honeymoon period, Petra's strict leadership style became apparent. She wanted to be number one. "Place the most students!" she'd repeat. "Do what you need to do!"

Petra didn't believe in "work smarter, not harder." She'd stay in the office into the evening and expected her staff to as well. I finally gathered that she had invited me out before the first day of work to solidify some sort of alliance with me as part of the "new guard." There was a history of upheaval in the office, and she wanted me to be on her side. I wasn't privy to the whole story, but it sounded messy.

Several months into the job, I became stymied by the frenetic student recruitment procedures and the ever-devolving office dynamic.

The US headquarters, located appropriately in DC took limitless applications for international students requesting to live abroad. As long as the students' families paid the application fee and related charges, the students were accepted. The problem: We didn't have unlimited American families lined up to take in these loveable adolescent multinational scholars, nicknamed LAMS. These unsuspecting students were casualties of the Several Leaders Advising Unreachable Goals to House Teens Everywhere, Recklessly. LAMS to the SLAUGHTER.

This meant students were temporarily placed in any home we could find, including our own. Yes, the regional office workers, me included, were pressured to take in students who didn't have families assigned to them, but who were put on a plane anyway.

It was reminiscent of the *Oprah Winfrey Show* episodes with car giveaways, but with unsuspecting, trusting youth. Imagine an Oprah-like figure with a booming voice pointing to each staff in the room: "You get a LAMS! And you get a LAMS! Everyone gets a LAMS!" Instead of the recipients shrieking in joy, however, we would cringingly consent and worry about having to feed, entertain, and emotionally support a foreign exchange student for an undetermined amount of time.

In the thick of the placement crisis, Cindy and her boyfriend agreed to host a student temporarily until a permanent home could be found. The young teen slept in their bed while they took the living room fold-out couch for at least a month.

Drew also gave in fairly quickly. I think she recruited her parents, who lived in the Chicago suburbs, to take in a student temporarily.

I was the last of the three of us to agree to this surprise add-on to our job description. A girl from New Zealand ended up sleeping on a futon in my sparsely furnished two-bedroom apartment for a couple of weeks. It felt awful—I didn't know any other teens she could hang out with.

Why wouldn't the office in DC accept students only on the contingency that they had a family awaiting them upon arrival? It would have prevented this debacle. It defies logic for me. I'm sure it boiled down to money. I know that a lot of host families and students had wonderful experiences. Unfortunately, as a full-time employee, I was instead mired in the less-than-ideal experiences, and it bothered me that upper management did not seem to offer a better system for all involved.

HOW WE THOUGHT IT WOULD FLOW:

1. DC provides profiles of international students (LAMS) to each regional office for placement based on host family availability in region
2. Paid regional employees help local volunteers with resources—trainings, strategies, etc. to assist host families
3. Host families welcome the LAMS to the US at the end of August with the support of local volunteers
4. Host families provide lodging, food, school registration, and transportation to LAMS as monitored by local volunteers
5. Students (LAMS) receive a rich cultural experience with the support of locals backed up by regional employees

REALITY: A SERPENTINE SAGA

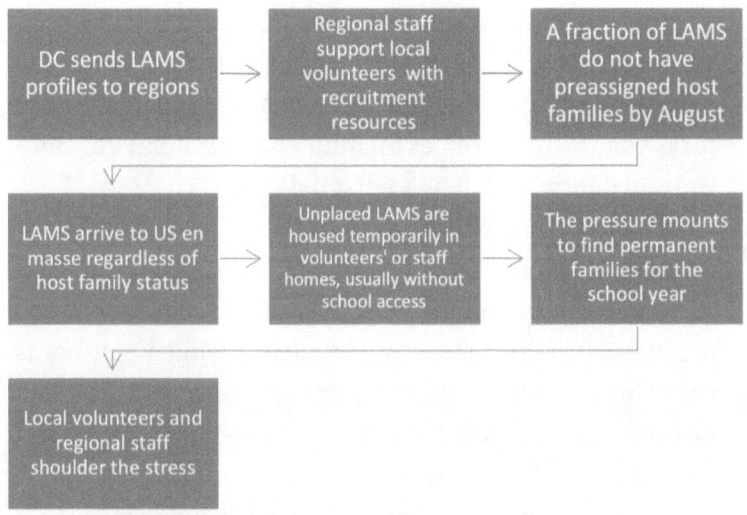

At first, the new guard—me, Cindy, and Drew—seemed to get along despite the stress.

Cindy had been in the Peace Corps. Very cool. She must have had a region in Wisconsin as well, or maybe she had all of Missouri. I can't recall. She had a liberal arts background similar to mine, making her as qualified (or as unqualified) as I was.

Drew had another region—mostly northern Illinois and Chicago. She had a degree in recreational science or physical education, something along those lines. She had a strong personality and instilled confidence, making her a ringleader of sorts. People were apt to follow her. However, despite her great verbal qualities and assertiveness, she couldn't write. She could not put a sentence together. Grammar, spelling, punctuation: all foreign concepts to her.

Our working relationship began to sour when, as a

group, we decided to put out a newsletter to the lead volunteers to help motivate them and keep them updated on what the regional office was up to. Drew did not use spellcheck. She seemed offended when I went to proofread the newsletter and pointed out some mistakes, such as "hissstory" for "history" or "exsitemint" for "excitement." Both she and Cindy took it as a personal attack.

I was a people pleaser most of the time—but not at the expense of an error-riddled publication with my name on it. I mean, I was well read and enjoyed a well-crafted turn of phrase. I couldn't just stand by silently while English was being butchered. I thought I was being nice about it—like "Great ideas! Let's just fix some of the spelling." No dice. I was blacklisted by Drew and the gang.

I had inklings my coworkers started disliking me before that. They seemed to think I was the director's favorite. I was the first of us three newbies to be hired by Petra, and I had recounted to them that she wanted to meet me for a drink before my first day of work. I thought confiding in my coworkers about this strange encounter would show I was on their side, lead us to commiserate about what a peculiar, unreasonable boss she was. Instead, they came to think I was in her pocket or something. They also probably resented that I was the last holdout on taking in a student. It felt crazy. I was only thirtyish. Too young to be a host mom, I thought. But, as mentioned, I did finally give in. I guess fixing the newsletter was the straw that broke the camel's back. Or was it the keystroke that destroyed the computer? Or the comma that spliced the sentence?

Within a few months of starting that job, I felt very much an outsider. Aside from the weird office dynamics, the pressure to prod and persuade volunteers to find host families, people living in a relatively distant community from my own, was awkward. They were volunteers. With no pay. They obviously signed up to help with the organization because they believed in the benefits of cultural exchange, but you can't force a family to house a LAMS for a year.

Placement issues continued throughout the year. Some students needed to leave a host family for one reason or another, often due to irreconcilable differences. Then began a quest to guilt another family into taking in a kid. For example, there was a European kid aghast at her host family's reliance on paper plates and plastic utensils to cut down on dishwashing, regardless of the environmental implications. Or the kid who didn't feel safe in a house where the couple fought constantly (we eventually learned the father was sneaking out all the time to have an affair). Some kids seemed entitled, or on the other end of the spectrum, very introverted, unable to adjust to a new cultural situation, no matter how kind and generous the family was.

After about twenty months, I called it quits. (Cindy and Drew were also disillusioned. Last I heard, Cindy went into massage therapy school, while Drew worked in accounts payable for a community recreation facility.) It seems none of us were willing to ride the wave and hope for better outcomes within this organization. Maybe the nonprofit was promoting world peace one family at a time in other regions, but in the Midwest, it felt more like we were putting out fires, trying to keep one step ahead of the chaos.

Even more disappointing was that I left that job without friendships or at least acquaintances who I might turn to for support from time to time. I was on my own again with only a skeletal social network. (This network mainly included Liam, and I still kept in touch occasionally with

Ellen, Winnie, and Crystal, who all lived within thirty to forty miles of Chicago.) But, as the saying goes, "Where there's life, there's hope."

My new plan: Go back to school for another master's degree, this time for Teaching English as a Second Language (TESOL), a field in applied linguistics. Inspired by my work in Dijon, I remembered enjoying using various linguistic artifacts in class to teach English. "That sounds like the rewarding work I've been seeking," I thought.

No small factor was my parents' approval. Specifically, my retired father had been a music professor who highly valued academics and teaching. Aside from the strong desire to maintain my independence and make my own way in the world, I really wanted to do something my parents would appreciate and be proud of.

I mused that there must be full-time work in this field in Chicago, a city of immigrants. I looked in the classifieds (long before searching jobs online was the norm) and saw a full-time job at College of DuPage for TESOL. Drawing the conclusion from just one ad that jobs would be plentiful (back to Bud Light status), I excitedly enrolled in a master's program in Chicago at age thirty. I'd be helping others, using my knowledge of what it's like to live abroad, learning about new cultures, and supporting the underdog. Finally, I had found the ideal career.

CHAPTER 5

First, Take My Money; Then Burst My Bubble

To incur less debt while earning my master's in linguistics, I taught French as a teaching assistant (TA)—one or two classes a semester—while attending classes full time.

I wasn't comfortable as a French TA. My fear that my French was inadequate came back to haunt me, which in hindsight is kind of ridiculous. I mean, I'd lived abroad twice and earned an advanced degree in French. But I forced myself in front of the classes every day because I'd accepted the job, and pride ruled. Gradually I became somewhat more acclimated, though never brimmed with confidence. Decades later, I still have occasional anxiety dreams about teaching French—forgetting to go to my class, being unprepared for the day's lesson, etc.

Despite being nervous as a TA—a setup probably similar to ESL teaching—I stuck to the narrative that I needed to teach ESL to adults. I thought being an ESL teacher would be a doable vocation. I assumed I could find a full-time position with mentorship and supportive, like-minded co-workers. While the public speaking aspect induced anxiety, I liked composing lesson plans, expanding on topics creatively, and even designing tests and rubrics for assessment.

I began applying for jobs in the last semester before graduating. When I asked one of my professors for a letter of recommendation for an out-of-state full-time position, she frowned at me, incredulous at my gullibility. She told me it's very unlikely to get a job in the field in any community in which you don't already live. I was newly single after my six-year off and on relationship with Liam finally ended (more on that later) and wanted a fresh start in a new career, either locally or elsewhere if necessary. At age thirty-two, I still had an adventurous spirit and hope for the future. But within that thirty-second exchange, weeks away from graduating with my second master's degree, my hopes were squashed.

As I did more research, her curt assessment of my job prospects panned out. Locally in Chicago, most ESL jobs were part-time. Most teachers patched together a living taking on several adjunct positions at a time. This meant working nights, weekends, afternoons—really any time slot where there was an open position. It was a profession of "pickers can't be choosers." It also meant the absence of benefits—specifically, health insurance. One of my classmates did get a full-time position at a downstate community college, but I think she had connections.

Though I thought I was willing to move for my job, I didn't want to move back to a small town like where I grew up. It sounded too isolating. Even my midsized college town had come to seem too small to me, a dead-end street. Though it never provided me the lifelong career opportunities I'd hoped for, the TESOL degree led to genuine friendships that continue to this day.

To be fair, most students went into the TESOL program with eyes wide open. Teaching English to adult immigrants for them was likely a passion, regardless of how many adjunct positions they had to piece together to make ends meet. It's a gig lifestyle, not dissimilar to musicians or consultants who are self-employed, assuming the burden of paying for their own health insurance.

Taking a cue from my fretful mother, though, I stuck to the narrative that I needed the whole shebang, a full-time salary and health care benefits. It was the safe choice. I couldn't imagine worrying each semester if I'd be rehired or able to pay all the bills. Hubris played into it somewhat; I had two master's degrees and felt entitled to more. Obviously, my ideal job didn't match the reality of the job market, especially given my eclectic qualifications. That was all. Blame for my distorted understanding of the job market cannot be justly placed on the instructors in the TESOL program.

Finally, two years after I started the program, no longer sure I could use it, I earned my master of science in linguistics in 2003. I was thirty-two and felt as ambivalent as ever about my ability to put down roots in both my professional and personal life.

SHADOW BOXER

Liam and I had begun seeing each other romantically again a month after I moved to Chicago. (After we broke up but before he moved there, I really thought we were just going to be friends.) We spent a lot of time together over those years in Chicago—dinner, movies, museums, weekend sleepovers. We once took a road trip to Canada with his friend Leo and Leo's girlfriend.[12] We even took a big trip out West a year before our final breakup.

But Liam never called me his girlfriend. We always had fun together, and I told myself I didn't need labels. I didn't want to rock the boat by asking too many questions or making emotional demands. It doesn't just sound pathetic; it is pathetic. Even more puzzling is that I identified as a feminist—believed women deserved equal pay and respect.

As I reflect some twenty years later, I understand I was too emotionally entrenched to see my situation as an antithesis to my beliefs. In retrospect, it makes sense, considering what I learned through observation as a child—that the males are the pioneers, the ones with agency (gag). Not challenging him about his real feelings for me felt safe, while confrontation felt unsafe. Ignorance was bliss—emotional bubble wrap. Sadly, I felt lucky to be accepted at all by a person as accomplished as Liam and held onto that connection like a lifeline.

I kept taking my cues from him and, like a shadow boxer,[13] managed to shift according to his various moves and moods, to adapt to his loose interpretation of our relationship. I basically entangled myself in a six-year, undefined relationship. I made few to no demands, and in return was crushed again into mincemeat months before graduating with my second master's degree. I needed to brush myself off and start a new chapter, but it was a heavy blow that stayed with me for a while. I tried to shift my focus back to my professional life, as much as possible, as a temporary balm.

---

12. Another fun fact: The trip was marred at first because my mother had insisted that I take a strong antibiotic after I made the mistake of offhandedly showing her a weird insect bite on my ankle. She was convinced I had Lyme disease. She promptly got a prescription for me through a doctor she knew. The lovely side effect was terrible constipation. I stopped taking it after a day. And guess what? I didn't actually have Lyme disease.
13. I love metaphors. Can you tell?

CHAPTER 6

Egomania

After graduating from the TESOL program, I spent early summer considering my options. I looked at positions within the university where I got my degree. Surely, if I couldn't teach full-time in my field and attain benefits, I could be of some use to academia in an administrative role.

In sum, I felt I had a lot of skills, and I just needed the chance to find the right niche. I didn't reflect on the mundane library association job in my mid-twenties where boredom crushed me. Instead, I recalled my more recent office jobs via Manpower after first arriving in Chicagoland, to supplement the part-time French teaching job I'd actually told my parents about. I was fairly busy in those office jobs, and the time went quickly.

I applied for, and was offered, an administrative assistant position within the College of Allied Health Sciences in a major university.[14] I was to be the assistant to Frank, a department head and well-known professor in his field. The position included all of the metaphorical bubble wrap I wished for—health benefits, vacation time, stability.

---

14. I'm being intentionally vague. The reader just needs to know it was a major university with big-shot professors.

My predecessor, Mike, was getting married and going back to school. He trained me for two days before he was out. As I understood it, a major responsibility was to help Frank coordinate the admissions program for international students applying to the master's program in his department. Another staff member oversaw admissions for US students—your run-of-the mill recent American college graduates applying to an advanced degree program. Again, that word "international" enticed me. Along with international admissions, I'd edit the department head's syllabus and help him manage his schedule.

Turns out, there wasn't that much to do. And this was a full-time job, 8:30-4:00. Frank was only in the building three or four days a week, and typically left for home by two or three in the afternoon. He probably needed only a part-time assistant, at best.

There was only a smattering of applicants for the international master's program. And processing the applications hardly took more than a half hour or so a day, when applications even came in. Editing Frank's syllabus took about ten minutes each semester. As far as his schedule, he had a Blackberry and seemed to manage his own appointments most of the time. Sometimes I ran out to get him lunch.

After a few weeks into the job, I asked him for more work. He had me alphabetize the books on his bookshelf. A good task for a fifth grader. Not a challenging or ongoing project.

To fill the time, I cleaned and recleaned my office, read all about the admissions requirements for degrees within the College of Allied Health Sciences, including that of occupational therapy. I would chat in passing with graduate students and get glimpses into their backgrounds and goals. I kept up on national and local news by surfing the net.

I later learned that my predecessor, Mike, was a computer whiz and had spent a lot of his time helping other faculty with computer issues—an unofficial job duty that, I suppose, ate up a lot of his time. Not only did I not have the skills to fix computers, but when Frank learned of Mike's good deeds shortly after I was hired, he was furious. He put a kibosh on any other faculty using *his* assistant for their own purposes. They regarded me as off-limits and were polite but kept their distance from me.

Frank revealed his oversized ego in other ways. He was in the middle of authoring a textbook at one point, and the editors had the audacity to change his wording. This upset him. Grad students and I were witness to his reaction—gesticulating wildly, he said to us, "You don't fuck with Michelangelo." Yes, he compared himself to Michelangelo. I. Just. Could. Not.

There were other off-putting parts of his personality. For example, he treated the computer support people like dirt. If something wasn't working, Frank thought raising his voice and/or belittling their efforts was an effective way of getting the job done. This team was mostly student workers who were also responsible for the technology in the dean's office across the street. They couldn't be in two places at once, and treating them poorly just seemed mean—a cheap way for him to throw his weight around.

I know he was a well-published professor who made many contributions to his field, but this didn't excuse his behavior. Witnessing him being a jerk to many of his underlings annoyed me. And I was bored out of my gourd, on a downward path of plummeting self-worth and growing despondency. I tried to look busy all day, feeling more fraudulent than flourishing. Was my position—and by extension I—just an accessory to Frank's ego?

When I resigned after a year to take another opportunity within the university, he was livid I quit after only a year and told me so. No one voluntarily leaves the great Frank Udelhoven. Um, yes. I did.

My new job: an administrative assistant to the director of the International Service Department, or ISD. There's that damned "international" theme again—when would I ever learn? Unfortunately, I'd soon learn that ISD could've as easily stood for "It's So Dysfunctional."

CHAPTER 7

A Process of Elimination

The International Service Department provided guidance and counseling for international students, faculty, and visiting scholars on how to maintain their visa status to remain in the US. Typically this involves a lot of forms, fees, and photocopies. Deadlines are important. In short, it's an office specializing in governmental red tape.

In the interview, I learned this particular office also organized periodic outings for international students, encouraged participation in multicultural events, and planned orientations, all on top of providing the baseline visa consultation services. I clung to these details, thinking this would be a rewarding position. In reality, though, I was only parenthetically involved in any of the fun stuff. The counselors who specialized in visa applications also planned and organized outings and other events.

I, on the other hand, was essentially a glorified (and overeducated) secretary, scheduling appointments for the director, Randall, ordering office supplies, and covering the front desk when the front desk clerk needed help or was on a break. There was always a big push in August and

September when new students arrived, where all hands were on deck. In that sense, I guess I was useful.

Randall was tightly wound. Once, when he was out of town on a weekday to help his daughter move into college, there was a water leak in one of the offices. Of course, we contacted maintenance. They cleaned up the mess and repaired the leak in the roof. When he returned to the office, Randall was incensed that we hadn't contacted him.

Another time, Randall got bent out of shape that we weren't exclusively using the new cross-cut paper shredding machine in place of the more basic one that cut paper in strips. I guess he thought ICE (US Immigration and Customs Enforcement) was watching him at all times. I'm sure there was incredible pressure on him to be immaculate in all visa procedures and policies in the aftermath of 9/11. But I think we all wanted to just say, "Christ Almighty! Chill out, Randy boy." I imagine such advice would not have been well received.

On paper, all full-time employees were allowed ten vacation days a year. In reality, asking for any more than a day off usually felt like diplomatic gymnastics. Most of us didn't ask for much vacation time. Before I accepted the position, I informed Randall that there was a day in August I'd have to miss to attend my brother's wedding. While he initially winced and frowned at my request, he granted it without further comment, which wasn't the case for everyone.

Camila, a visa counselor working mainly with students, was originally from Mexico, and, incidentally, was the only non-Caucasian employee in the office. In confidence, she shared with me and a few other coworkers that she'd privately requested five days off to get married and honeymoon in Mexico, which Randall approved. She'd purposely planned it during February, a quieter time for the department.

After she returned from Mexico, Randall lorded this over her. "You really owe me," I overheard him say to her. "You're not getting time off again anytime soon." That floored me: It was her wedding, a once in a lifetime event (hopefully). I didn't understand why he'd want her to feel guilty about it. I wondered, "Did I misunderstand his tone? Was he joking?"

I delicately approached Camila in private afterwards to see if she was OK. She replied stoically that she was fine. She'd had a wonderful time in Mexico, but she was ready to get back to work. Maybe Randall's comments didn't really bother her. Regardless, she was astute enough to not make any waves, to stay on Randall's good side to preserve her job.

Despite the undercurrent of tension permeating the office, I held onto a faint hope of getting more responsibility. Translation: more challenging work and a sense that my efforts had value. After several months into the job, Randall indicated he needed help with data management to track the budget, and that I should get some training on the university's data management software system. I attended multiple trainings, but he never gave me access to files that would allow me to perform these duties. It was very puzzling.

My lasting impression of Randall is that of an uptight, middle-aged bureaucrat lacking transparency and any *joie de vivre*. How do you appease a boss who doesn't communicate with you? Then there was me, people pleasing and lacking confidence to express my concerns. Not a great dynamic. Still, I think if he had sat down with me and outlined clearly what additional work he needed from me, I would have complied. But I wasn't the only one that Randall didn't jell with easily.

Apart from Randall's critical, close scrutiny of time-off requests and various everyday minutia, there were other red flags that I turned a blind eye to. From day one, Randall spoke disparagingly, behind her back, of Vivian, the front desk clerk. He could not outright fire her because she belonged to the civil servants' union (the only union employee in the office). He soon got her transferred to another office in the student services building, with the support of the dean. After she was transferred, he turned his attention to another employee for target practice.

Also a veteran employee and visa counselor at the International Service Department, Marge was friendly and outgoing, with sort of a hippie vibe to her. Her style of dress was somewhat bohemian, in an office environment where most people either wore suits, blazers, or at least business casual.

I did my best to keep a polite distance from her, as it was clear that Randall didn't care for her. The dean appeared to work with Randall to transfer her to another position within the university several months after my arrival, in the study abroad office within a different building. Two down, Vivian and Marge. I should have asked, "Who's next?" but nay (neigh?), my blinders were on.

When Randall decided to create a new position requiring specialized visa experience, Lydia, another longtime visa counselor, applied for the job. She thought she was a shoo-in. Once she did apply, he seemed to turn against her—apparently convinced not only that she didn't possess the full qualifications, but that she wasn't even trainable for this advanced position. It was sad—she was surprised at the formality of the interview, and the subsequent snub. Shortly after this souring experience, she understandably applied elsewhere and left. He was really shaking up the core staff.

THE TESOL TRIAL

As I puzzled over my role in the department, trying to fit in socially and derive a sense of purpose from the work, I still felt disappointed with myself that I'd not used my TESOL degree at all. I'd had the degree a whole year at that point. I mused, "Maybe I could teach one night class to get my feet wet, work my way into the system. Who knows?" I continued, "It could lead me to that ever-elusive unicorn—a full-time job with benefits that requires the skills from my latest master's degree."

With this Panglossian reasoning, I accepted a community college ESL position teaching a three-hour class, four nights a week several months after starting at the international services job. The class would be about twenty students.

Provided up front with the students' fluency level and the class textbook and workbooks, I spent the two weeks before the class started carefully planning out lessons for at least the first week, following the curriculum I was given.

I was nervous but, again, felt this was the necessary step to doing work that was meaningful to me. I was sticking to this narrative: It would complement my full-time administrative job that provided health care benefits.

On the first day of class, prepared and ready to go as best I could, I was told that due to enrollment and staffing issues, the department coordinator had combined two classes into one. The class size doubled. I would be teaching two levels of students in one class. They gave me a different textbook to use, and all my planning up was now largely unusable.

Dumbfounded and nearly paralyzed with anxiety, I stumbled into that first class of forty-some students with my icebreaker activity and intro lessons, based on the original curriculum, and designed for twenty people. Walking away would have been understandable, but such an option didn't enter my mind. I felt I'd made the commitment and needed to stick with it.

A well-seasoned teacher can fairly easily adapt to any number of unexpected circumstances. I was—spoiler alert—not well-seasoned. On top of that, many students arrived late and/or had spotty attendance both that night and throughout the term. I did my best to get through that first night and power through the rest of the semester. It was nearly impossible to learn everyone's name. How does anyone provide quality instruction to students with inconsistent attendance? Oh, and they didn't do homework. They had other responsibilities outside of class—jobs, kids, etc.—homework wasn't high on their priority list.

Still, I tried to implement some creative ideas to motivate the students. One project I designed was to have the students study clips of Siskel and Ebert, the famous film critics who had their own TV show. As a class, we analyzed the language they used to agree or disagree. I gave them a template and word bank, and asked them to team up with a partner to critique a film or TV show in the style of Siskel and Ebert.

Another theme was technology and gadgets, so I brought in some gadgets from home and, in small groups, had them guess the purpose of each gadget for a speaking/

vocabulary lesson. I could have just followed the textbook, I guess, but that wasn't best practice.

Despite being nervous and a wreck at the end of each week, wringing my hands at both my day and night jobs, I gave it my all for fifteen weeks, ending a couple of weeks before Christmas. Exhausted, I hung up my TESOL hat for a while. It was time to imbibe in some festive beverages, pop in some classic holiday DVDs (National Lampoon's *Christmas Vacation* comes to mind), and hunker down as much as possible for the rest of that seasonably harsh Chicago winter.

Even without the stress of the night job, conditions did not ameliorate during my day job. There aren't really many funny stories from my time at international services. I tried to muster up bubbly enthusiasm and joke with coworkers, in hopes of inserting myself into the more humanizing aspects of the office (such as planning outings and intermingling with the international students), to no avail. I went on at least one outing, to the Morton Arboretum, but the other employees remained merely cordial to me, certainly not close. One visa counselor was a thirty-something man—well spoken, educated, with a good sense of humor. Then one day he casually mentioned, without a hint of humor, his current topic of leisure time research—he was reading up on the rapture, the ascent into heaven for the "chosen" after the coming apocalypse. He seemed to take it seriously. Not my cup of tea.

Finally, it was my turn to sport a target on my back. After around one year in the job, I got to join the good company of the other coworkers who had been pushed out before me:

Vivian, Marge, and Lydia. It was a Friday morning. I arrived at work at 8 a.m. as usual. Opening the door to my office area, I was stunned. My desk was gone, along with my office supplies. In their place were several file cabinets.

Randall spied me through the window separating my office space from the front office, where he was chatting with a couple of office staff. He strolled into my "space" and announced matter-of-factly that I would now be stationed at the front desk. He abruptly walked out after sharing that riveting news, offering no further explanation.

A few moments later, trembling, I made my way to his office, located in an office suite beyond the front desk area. He was flipping through some papers on his desk and looked up dispassionately as I stood in his doorway. I asked him plainly, "Randall, please, just tell me what I did wrong. I don't understand!" He didn't answer. Do you know the expression "resting bitch face?" He just sat there with his "resting constipation face." I walked away shell shocked and confused.

After a week or two at the front desk, feeling humiliated and underrated, I accepted a transfer to the Career Services Office upstairs within the same building. This was a small concession. It allowed me to stay on the university payroll but away from Randall. He was visibly thrilled—my pay no longer came from his budget. When he learned I was transferring, his step was lighter, and the motherfucker had a beaming smile on his face. I guess reducing department expenses was his Metamucil.

At the Career Services Office, the other employees were welcoming to me but, again, I just answered phones and shuffled paper, no more than a student worker would do. The irony wasn't lost on me—I was sub-employed, working beneath my abilities and underchallenged in an office whose sole purpose was to counsel university students in their career search. I felt empty and shiftless. Another failed job.

One evening, I pulled out of my parking space and accidentally backed into a utility pole, invisible in the heavy snowfall. I was so depressed that, though I banged up my rear bumper, I didn't stop to report it or get out to ask for help. I drove silently out of the parking lot into the white, still evening, wondering the point of it all.

CHAPTER 8

Hyphens, Italics, and Commas—Oh, My!

In the evenings at home, I scoured the classifieds religiously. I still held to the narrative that I needed a job with health insurance; teaching ESL was off my radar as those jobs in Chicagoland were all part-time without benefits. After a week or two, I had a lightbulb moment and wondered if there were any local jobs in publishing.

I recalled that one of my TESOL instructors mentioned he'd worked in publishing for a while before he began teaching ESL. This was funny to me and my fellow students, as his syllabi always contained several obvious typos. I mused that maybe he'd exhausted all interest in that career and the typos were an intentional "screw you" to his former profession. Still, editing sounded like a job I could do. And despite no real experience in the business, it seemed like a safe, bubble-wrap-type move—an office job with health insurance.

I rationalized further: My written communication skills had always been a strength. As an undergraduate and graduate student, I produced thoughtful and original essays on multiple topics, from historical fiction to French lit analyses. In a film class, I was particularly proud of an analysis of two Jean Renoir films that I compared through the lens of imprisonment and freedom, both concrete and metaphorical. Academic writing was my jam!

The writing process represented a satisfying intellectual pursuit for me in higher education. Don't get me wrong—it also got stressful when faced with deadlines and intermittent self-doubt. Editing my own work was the easier step of the writing process. It was the opportunity to polish and refine my thoughts. With this in mind, I speculated that the publishing industry held real potential for me in terms of career development.

Above all, I wanted desperately to be away from the university community that, in my mind, radiated toxicity.

Lo and behold, during my ritual combing of the job classifieds, I came across an ad for an editorial assistant at a company publishing educational and technical materials, such as textbooks for vocational programs in community colleges and technical colleges.

The interview was surprisingly thorough: a phone interview, followed by an in-person timed editing test, capped off by an interview with the editor-in-chief. The editor-in-chief was impressed with me, but asked me directly if this is what I wanted, as it had nothing to do with French. I replied that I was excited to try a new career path. I was hired about a month before my thirty-fifth birthday.

After I learned the ropes, I continued to hold out for a sense of satisfaction and fulfillment. The daily work, unfortunately, wasn't as intellectually robust as I'd hoped. What does an editorial assistant do in this firm?

Let's say the academic writing process is akin to planning and executing a gourmet meal. You plan all stages of the meal, from the appetizer to the main course, as well as the dessert and aperitif. You pick out the ingredients carefully and present the meal with care.

To me, editing technical copy was like microwaving a frozen, ready-to-eat meal. Sure, there's some skill involved in this task. You have to be alert enough to follow the correct sequence: peel the corner, microwave on high for 3 mins, stir, microwave 1 more min, and let sit for 1 min. But you don't get to choose the ingredients, the composition of the meal. An editorial assistant makes sure the basic grammar is correct, terms and spelling are consistent (naïve instead of naive), and conventions are constant throughout a work—should we italicize this, or bold that?

Missing is the satisfaction of contributing to any of the content—not that I knew anything about the topics, such as computer programming, electricity, and plumbing. The material was dry to me. The daily tasks were boring (to me).[15] The office was as quiet as a cemetery, designed intentionally to screen out distractions. We couldn't have beverages at our desks or play music quietly. Breaks were relegated to twice a day, fifteen minutes in the morning and afternoon. Signs of life were highly discouraged.

Did I mention the pay? It was barely a livable wage, which means I couldn't put away any money in savings. In the meantime, upper management drove expensive cars and took off occasional afternoons to golf. The good old boys' vibe got on my nerves.

The long commute didn't help. From my humble apartment in the city, a little west of downtown, it took about one hour to drive each way. Numerous variables might extend that time, from a few raindrops to car accidents

---

15. No doubt this was not everyone's experience. A blanket apology to all fulfilled editorial assistants out there.

and road construction. I was exhausted and stressed before even making it into work. Once home, I wanted to shovel food into my mouth, and, ideally, eke out a little time for something I enjoyed—reading, watching a rental from Blockbuster (retro alert!), cuddling with my two cats, or meeting up with a few friends for pub trivia or a bite to eat.

I eventually moved to a neighborhood farther south, Hyde Park, but the commute was still long enough to be unpleasant. I was initially thrilled to be blocks from Lake Michigan. However, a peaceful walk by the sparkling, vast lakefront, with the downtown skyline in the distance, doesn't necessarily quiet all worries. Instead, it was, more often, a cruel reminder that the wondrous promises of the Big City seemed, tauntingly, always just out of my reach.

I became friendly with a couple of coworkers at the publishing firm, but the nature of the work left little time for collaboration or socializing. There was a clique of young women who were gossipy and snarky during coffee and lunch breaks. This really depressed me. They reminded me of my high school days, a time I didn't fit in with any clique, and ate my lunch in the library, alone. The silence in that job was deafening, the solitude stifling.

Importantly, I was as far away from winning my parents' approval as possible. My dad actually asked me at one point if I, myself, was publishing any of my own work at this job. I was confused—he knew I was a low-level editorial assistant. It was a passive-aggressive attack on my lack of success. At that point, my brother had long since earned his PhD and was working steadily in academia. I felt light years away from fulfilling any meaningful role in society, let alone being a star of academia. The only worse job, in my dad's eyes, would have been a banker. He figured all bankers were Republican, money-grubbing scum. At least I wasn't a banker![16]

As an aside, a few years later after my life took yet more turns, I became a co-author of a textbook used to train students being certified to teach English abroad. I wrote three chapters myself, co-authored another chapter, and edited the whole thing.

But by the time the textbook bearing my name was ready to go to press, my father's health was in rough shape. He had developed congestive heart failure and was struggling to recover in a rehabilitation facility after two weeks in the hospital. Sadly, my dad had lost his usual spark and witty repartee. He was on oxygen and faded in and out of alertness. During one of my many visits, a three-hour drive from my home, I tried to show him the chapters I wrote—the content included inside jokes and subtle references to our family, which I hoped he'd appreciate. But he couldn't stay alert long enough to read it or even acknowledge my accomplishment. I like to think if he had had his wits about him, he'd have been proud of this small feat. He died a few months later at age ninety, having lived a full, rich life.[17]

PURA VIDA: A BREATH OF FRESH AIR VOLUNTEERING IN COSTA RICA

Dissatisfied with the daily grind of publishing, after a year in the job, I sought a reprieve in a ten-day "volunteer vacation" program in Costa Rica. I had to pay for my flight, a

---

16. Again, a blanket apology to all bankers who are NOT money-grubbing scum. The rest of you are probably too busy with your yachts and mansions to feel slighted.
17. My dad lived a life filled with more light than shadow. His long life encompassed many roles including esteemed music professor, loyal husband and father, doting pet owner, and an unapologetic, staunch, liberal Democrat.

program fee, and any extra tours and sightseeing, but room and board were provided in exchange for volunteering five to six hours daily for a community project. After hosting a small fundraiser (which is encouraged, even though it felt weird), I cut travel costs in half.[18]

The community project assignment involved looking after at least thirty-five children of all ages living in a foster home. They had a wide range of needs. Some were typically developing but struggling emotionally. Others had physical or cognitive challenges. Though termed foster children, they were really permanent residents of this loving home.

There were fifteen to twenty volunteers on the trip. Some worked with the older kids to teach them English or show them how to help with housework. I chose to work with several of the younger kids, reading them stories (in my novice Spanish), walking with them to the playground, and fixing small meals. I loved it. One little boy, no more than three or four, became attached to me, and I felt for him. It was heartbreaking to see so many kids in need, but equally heartwarming to see how they all looked out for one another, and to know they were in a safe, loving environment. They took turns on the swing without complaint, and noticed if one of their peers fell down or needed help in any way.

On top of the volunteer work, there were a few excursions built into the experience, such as visiting a volcano, hiking through a rainforest, and visiting an art museum in nearby San Jose. It was a fun balance of sightseeing,

---

18. My mother, the ever-vigilant nurse and mother, was convinced that I needed malaria medicine for this trip. But I checked with my doctor, and the CDC (Centers for Disease Control and Prevention) did not recommend malaria precautions for this part of Costa Rica. I lied to my mother, saying I was taking the medicine. I finally learned that withholding information from her was, at times, the best way to protect her.

tasting local cuisine, and getting to know the community, if ever so briefly.

After my Costa Rican adventure, it was life as usual back at ye olde publishing company. The contrast was stark. I had just spent ten days volunteering with children, learning about a new culture, practicing my novice Spanish, and sampling new food. Upon my return, I had to resume the antiseptic, sedentary, and largely solitary work of copy editing, bookended by a long daily commute by car.

In my second year in publishing, at age thirty-six, I received a promotion to copy editor with a slight increase in pay, with a slight shift in responsibilities. The bosses did offer me a few new opportunities—learning to create indices and tackling a cooking textbook, with content more relatable than, say, plumbing. Still, the silence, isolation, and daily minutiae conspired to suffocate me. The editing job droned on.

Tedious times called for decisive action. My options: Continue to slowly sink into boredom or engineer a lifeboat. There had to be another way.

CHAPTER 9

OT Doesn't Mean Overtime, But It Was About Time

SEEDS OF CHANGE

Fueled by my discontentment as a technical copy editor, I dared to contemplate a major career change. At first, yet another graduate degree seemed both foolish and daunting. But the more I researched the field of occupational therapy (OT), the more realistic it seemed.

I had originally learned about OT during my stint working in the College of Allied Health Sciences. While I worked for Frank, I had a lot of free time on my hands. During that yearlong tenure as Frank's assistant, I systematically pored through the admissions catalogues that described the various allied health professions. Degrees in these fields were highly marketable, and it amused me to imagine an alternate reality, one in which I could go back in time and choose a different, more viable career path. It helped to pass the time.

Nutrition science looked interesting, but the curriculum included hard-core chemistry and physics classes. I was strong in neither. Plus, I'd rather savor food than analyze it for nutritional value. Kinesiology/exercise science sounded like it might attract jocks—no thanks. The program for certified nursing assistants (CNAs) conjured images of regular exposure to blood and other bodily fluids. I admired CNAs' compassion and dedication to their patients, but such work definitely wasn't for me.

Occupational therapy, though, charmed me. I ran into a few OT students over that year and, in passing, learned more about the field. They all had inspiring stories as to why they wanted to enter the profession.

One student, Jessica, had watched her older sibling recover from a traumatic brain injury in large part due to intensive OT.

Another student, Rachel, had a cousin with autism. Once nonverbal and aggressive as a toddler, her cousin was now a flourishing middle schooler thanks largely to private therapies, OT included.

Maria, yet another student, had no personal history with major medical trauma. Her enthusiasm for OT originated in seeing her mother thrive as a school-based OT, mainly working with young children.

There was even a male OT student, Sebastian (affectionately called a "Bro-T" by his female classmates). His interest in OT was piqued after he volunteered, as an undergraduate psychology major, with dementia patients in a nursing home where OTs ran weekly exercise groups.

According to the informational brochures, admissions catalogues, and testimonials by the OT students, this discipline valued creativity, social justice, and holistic treatment of patients. All of these values aligned with my personal beliefs. Plus, according to my research, all signs pointed to excellent job prospects for occupational therapists in the foreseeable future, as well as decent pay across the board.

OK, enough with the "OTs are amazing" speech.

Though impressed by the positives, I initially assumed this field was out of my reach, given that I hadn't taken any real science courses since high school biology. The OT curriculum included courses in anatomy, physiology, and neuroscience, which all sounded intimidating. I thought instead, though, that *maybe* I could train to be a certified occupational therapy assistant (COTA). They practice in the same settings but aren't qualified to conduct evaluations and must be supervised by an OT.

To further research the field, I looked up programs that offered COTA certification. After locating a program in the south suburbs near the publishing firm, I scheduled an appointment right after work with a COTA who taught at this program. She was encouraging. With my background, she asserted, I'd be valuable in the profession.

"You're well-rounded," she said, "and your humanities background would be looked on favorably." She continued, "But you wouldn't be satisfied as a COTA—the OT degree takes about the same amount of time. As a full OT, you'd be more autonomous and get better pay."

I was surprised, but thrilled, that occupational therapy was emerging as a viable career option.

After that interview, I researched the prerequisites for an OT master's program. I spied a few academic hurdles. Despite all of my education, I was missing a few academic prerequisites for admissions to an OT program, including biology, abnormal psychology, anatomy and physiology, and statistics. While still working in the drudgery of copy editing, I enrolled in an introductory biology class and abnormal psych class at a downtown city college to get started.

I shared my plans with my parents, of course.

My mom's reaction was mildly supportive. Maybe she was thinking, "My well-intentioned but aimless daughter. Here she goes again." Or perhaps I'm projecting my own insecurities. I know, despite her anxiety about my physical safety, she did want me to be happy.[19]

My dad's reaction was kind of negative, like, "Why would you want to do that?" I don't think he fully understood the many positive aspects of this field, or he didn't want to. He understood languages, music, and literature, and had always wanted me to pursue an intellectual path. Perhaps he just didn't tune in to how miserable I was on my current trajectory. But his doubts didn't knock me down as they might have years earlier—somehow, I knew what I was doing. I was, to be trite, following my heart, and finally pushing others' approval to the back burner.

CAUTION TO THE WIND

Toward the end of the semester, the day of my biology final, I had planned to work all day as usual, drive home, and take the bus downtown to take the exam. But before noon that day, a wave of discomfort washed over me, and I felt

---

19. Actually, my mother always tended to express enthusiasm for even my minor talents and accomplishments. "You're such a good typist!" and "Wow, your word processing skills are amazing!" and "You can really read people." When her dementia became more dominant, especially after my dad died, my accomplishments became more inflated. "You are so great with all those languages!" she would say, even though my skills were limited to French and some beginning Spanish. She had such a positive, enthusiastic spirit that I wish could have appreciated more fully when I was younger.

like I couldn't breathe well. I was restless. Though I didn't recognize it as such at the time, I now understand this to have been a fairly major panic attack.

I decided to go home and told management I was coming down with something. I thought, "I'll just eat a good lunch, relax a bit, and feel better." But the unwell feeling continued.

Contributing to my discontent, several weeks prior, Casper, who I'd been dating for nine months, ghosted me. Disappeared. I was carrying a lot of emotional baggage.

I took my final that evening, ready to enroll in anatomy/physiology and statistics the next semester.

I realized a few days later, after speaking to my counselor, Barb (who I'd started seeing regularly after the Casper debacle), that I had probably experienced a prolonged panic attack.[20] It made sense—I had experienced a visceral reaction to the perpetual discontentment experienced at my day job.

The panic attack was my body's way of telling me—enough. Enough with the two-hour daily commute. Enough of silently enduring a job that makes you miserable. I had kept this stress bottled up long enough. When there's a will, there's a way.

Within a few weeks, almost thirty-seven years old, I had cobbled together two or three part-time TESOL jobs, quit the publishing job, and bought my own (crappy) health insurance. Fortunately, when I quit, I learned that since the company was employee-owned, I was entitled to a sizable chunk of cash—about $5,000. It was a pleasant surprise and much needed.

---

20. I met with Barb, a family counselor in Hyde Park, two to four times a month for about a year. It helped to have a sympathetic, objective listener during this rocky, uncertain time.

At this fork in the road, I visualize myself turning into a Hulk of sorts. After many months of mounting tension and despondency over my current job, I finally wake up to the absurdity of my situation and develop extraordinary strength to tackle the barriers making me miserable. The panic attack was the final straw. Bound by layers of bubble wrap, surrounded by baby gates and child safety locks, I rip off the bubble wrap and kick down the baby gates, tearing off the safety locks as I flee. I spring forward unencumbered, a trail of detritus behind me, finally throwing caution to the wind.

I continued to enroll in the classes I needed to apply to OT grad programs and taught English as a second language and college writing within well-established programs in the Chicago area.

CHAPTER 10

From Shadow to Light

With all the changes afoot, around the time I quit my copyediting job, I took on one more challenge. I decided to give dating one more try. Wary and skeptical, my expectations were low. "One more bad experience," I thought, "and I'm issuing a moratorium on dating. It's not worth the emotional drain."

With this mindset, I met Nico via a free dating website. Though I lived in Hyde Park, we met in my previous neighborhood, at an independent coffee shop. His condo was north of the city, in Des Plaines. Formerly a jazz saxophonist and community college instructor in music, Nico currently taught ESL to second graders. We talked a lot about teaching and travel on that "meet and greet."

We didn't see each other again for a couple of weeks because of the Thanksgiving holiday, but he emailed me quick messages in the interim, like "Eat that turkey." (This was prior to texting.) Nico, I learned, does not mince words.

We had another date in Chinatown watching the Chinese New Year parade and sampling some dim sum. The week after that, we toured the Robie House (the Frank Lloyd

Wright house near the University of Chicago) and went out for Thai food. It was going well. No drama.

We were engaged secretly after six months.[21]

On April first, he proposed to me while we relaxed on a bench in the Lincoln Park Zoo, not far from the camel and zebra enclosure, and a few more steps from the African apes. He offered me a jumbo, plastic purple ring that looked like it had come out of a gumball machine. I tried it on, distractedly inspecting the high-quality plastic design.

I winced and thought, "Did he belong on the other side of the animal enclosures? Were the zebras or, more likely, the apes minus a family member?"

"April Fools!" he exclaimed. And then he produced a real engagement ring (that I had picked out). He was not a player like Liam, nor a flake like Casper. Nico was a good guy.

Within a little over two years, I completed the academic prerequisites and applied to a Chicago area occupational therapy program that had a part-time option, making it more financially feasible.

I didn't apply anywhere else.

Several programs required experience in a cadaver lab, which I didn't have. Applying to one program was a leap of faith—all my eggs were in one basket. Finally, in spring 2011, a few days after sitting on the waitlist, and a week before my fortieth birthday, I was admitted to the Chicago-area program for a master's track occupational therapy program. I started in June, just a couple of weeks before I married Nico.

---

21. Though I shared the news with a few closer Chicago friends, still embarrassed by the drama with Casper, I waited a few more months to tell my family.

NOT ALL RAINBOWS AND BUTTERFLIES

Graduate school at any age is challenging. It's not meant to be a walk in the park.

Working part-time teaching ESL, attending classes with a much younger cohort, and acclimating to living with a new spouse in his tiny apartment—while trying to purchase a house—added to the stress.[22]

In the first two months, living even temporarily in a messy, cluttered one-bedroom condo with my new husband and my two cats was discouraging. I said to myself a few times, "My life was better before this."

Thankfully, we soon moved to a sublet in Ravenswood, a neighborhood not far from Wrigley Field, after Nico sold his condo. It was a cute apartment, but we slept on an air mattress while most of our furniture was in storage; we hoped to soon make an offer on a house.

A few uninvited roommates made their appearance after about ten days—baby cockroaches in the kitchen. "Aw, look at those cute baby cockroaches," we'd joke. Better to laugh than to cry.

If, as a couple, you can live through the house-buying process together, while staying in a cockroach-infested apartment, and while one of you is starting a new graduate program, you can probably endure almost anything.

We did indeed make it through—we found a house about five months after the wedding—with just a few metaphorical bumps and bruises. It was nice to have a partner, a home—to finally feel I'd put down roots.

---

22. Before we married, I had been living in a relatively spacious apartment on the north side of the city, close to the train to commute downtown for work but also a fairly convenient drive to Nico's place. When my lease ended and we got married, it seemed logical to move in together.

FRUITS OF LABOR, BITTERSWEET

A few weeks after earning my OT degree, I took the qualifying exam in January 2015, passing the first go-around. Three months shy of my forty-fourth birthday, it was a bittersweet commencement. My dad passed away in 2013, after I got married, but before I graduated.

Right after my dad passed away, we moved my mom to a nearby assisted living facility. Though I was employed as an OT before she passed away in 2017, dementia prevented her from fully understanding what I was doing. I do think she'd get a kick out of my career, especially the creative aspects—creating games and other activities to help kids reach their full potential.

While credit goes to both parents for my work ethic, I inherited the caring gene from my mom. Push aside the anxiety and worry that plagued her—she didn't choose those afflictions. I prefer to remember her for how she chose to treat other people. My mom set an example of how to be patient and caring, integral in working with children. She really did want me to do something that makes me happy—she thought teaching was the ticket.

The OT profession requires such skills, too—a lot of teaching goes into working effectively with clients, as well as other team members, such as administrators and caregivers. But apparently, I had to reach that decision on my own, and on my own terms.

Since 2015, I've been fully employed working with children, mainly in the public school system. It has its ups and downs, but it is never boring! And there are endless opportunities to think creatively, employ my writing skills, collaborate with others, and support children and their families struggling with a number of challenging circumstances.

While students I work with are not technically "international," many of the children are English language learners whose parents are relatively new to the US. On the downside, the paperwork required in public schools rivals that of most government agencies. (Jealous, ISD?) It's a lot to keep track of.

Any given workday may involve several of the following on this non-exhaustive list:

- Teaching preschoolers to hold and cut with adaptive scissors
- Setting up an obstacle course to improve students' balance, strength, and coordination
- Playing a DIY space-themed board game with a first grader for handwriting practice (because he loves the planets and is motivated by anything space-related)
- Leading a game of "feed the frog" with tweezers, pom-pom balls, and frog fashioned out of a tissue box to help young students develop finger strength
- Researching the best intervention techniques for a particular child
- Writing evaluations, progress reports, or discharge reports
- Running around the school to get to a meeting, make copies, touch base with a teacher, or collect some additional student data

You get the idea. It's a busy job. There are ups and downs, but time flies.

Doubtlessly there was a learning curve at the beginning, and it took me time to feel more comfortable in the role. Meetings with parents triggered my performance anxiety at first (now less so)—even though parents are typically respectful and appreciative.

Sure, some difficult facets of the job persist. There are the annoying mundane issues, like rarely having an area to store my supplies or a designated treatment space in most schools. You have to be flexible and resilient, which I can still manage after all these years.

More serious are the unusually difficult behavioral situations.[23] Fortunately, taking continuing education workshops and having supportive colleagues helps me to stay on top of my game.

I haven't regretted this decision. Despite the challenges, this career continues to tick all the boxes for me. The weird shadows, or fragments, of my past experiences somehow fit together now to form a more cohesive picture.

It was a long and winding road. The darkest shadows, by some saving grace, finally seem to reside safely in the rearview mirror.

---

23. Behavioral issues typically involve the children, but there is the occasional adult temper tantrum as well. I'll leave it at that.

Shadows of My Future Self

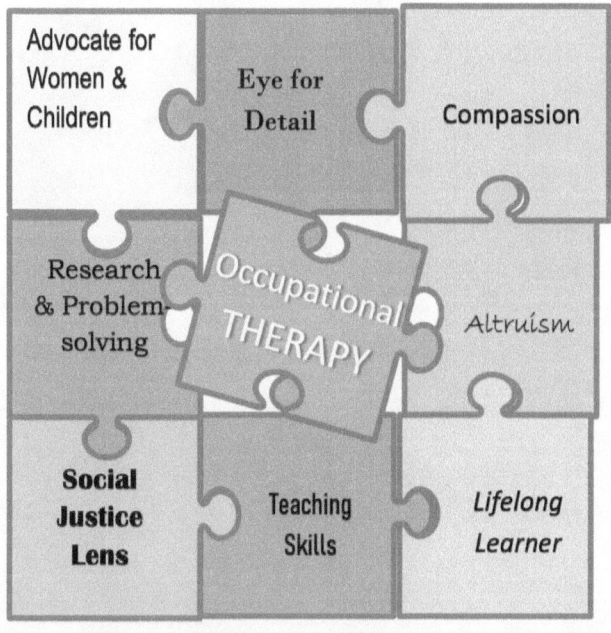

CHAPTER 11

Pithy Takeaways

"The first problem for all of us, men and women, is not to learn. It is to unlearn."
—GLORIA STEINEM

Steinem was likely referring to preconceived notions about traditional gender roles and equality of the sexes. Her remark can also apply to unlearning a variety of self-limiting beliefs that we adopt at a young age, either consciously or unconsciously. It's about changing our previously unquestioned narrative.

"Everybody has to fight to be free."
—TOM PETTY, FROM *REFUGEE*

Independence and freedom are not passive, smooth pursuits. They require perseverance through obstacles and resilience. Rock on, Tom Petty! (And R.I.P.)

"Hypotheticals are futile."
—ME

I'm sure there are plenty of readers of various fields, from comedians to lawyers, musicians to doctors, doing what they set out to do from a young age. But even these readers may be able to relate with my story on another level. Even if you've always done what you love, there are decisions you may have second-guessed, opportunities you've passed up.

The "what-ifs" can push me into a treacherous rabbit hole of hypotheticals. What if my mother had gotten a handle on her anxiety, and my dad his temper, and together they fostered reasonable risk-taking over fear of the unfamiliar? What if my parents outwardly celebrated girls' potential rather than tacitly endorsing outdated patriarchal tenets? Traveling back to my withdrawn adolescence, what if I'd gotten quality guidance from a watchful, competent school counselor to work on both my social skills and career exploration? What would my life be like now if I hadn't spent so much time on dead-end jobs? Conversely, would a smooth road to a degree in OT at the young age of twenty-two, without much life experience, have resulted in me being mediocre OT lacking the empathy I have now?

How much we evolve—or stagnate—both personally and professionally, is impacted by a myriad of factors, many beyond our control. Examples may include:

- formative experiences (both edifying and traumatic)
- family dynamics
- support system
- financial resources
- health
- educational opportunities
- discrimination (i.e., sexism, racism, homophobia, etc.) and
- the quality/visibility of role models

Clearly, we shouldn't waste time beating ourselves up over the past, especially when some hurdles are only overcome with time and perspective. Yes, the "what-ifs" are futile.

Of course, there have been many late bloomers in history, such as Vincent van Gogh, my favorite artist. He didn't start painting until he was twenty-seven. He struggled to find his way, and dabbled as an art dealer, bookseller, language teacher, and evangelist preacher. Unlike my old boss Frank, I'm not comparing myself to a famous artist, but there's something reassuring, even redemptive, about knowing I'm not alone in my meandering trajectory.

In addition—and I'm not saying anything new here—the shadows, whatever they may be for each of us, help to make us who we are.

CHAPTER 12

Final Takeaways, Frenchy Style

OR

You Can Take the Girl Out of the French Lit, But You Can't Take the French Lit Out of the Girl*

*Warning—The following contains subjective discussion of French literature. Not suitable for all audiences. Reader discretion advised.[24]

One of my favorite French poems, *Hommage à la vie*, by Jules Supervielle, wasn't even on any of my course syllabi. In fact, for all I know, it may be dismissed by the great professors as too trite. I ran across it in an old anthology of French poetry I bought for $3.50 in a used bookstore sometime in the '90s. Here are some favorite lines that seem apt:

---

24. If you are allergic to poetry or anything French, you may want to either skim this section quickly or skip it entirely. Au contraire, if you're into it, you may want to don a beret, slice a baguette, and enjoy it with a glass of wine or shot of espresso.

Original excerpts:	My attempt at translation:
Hommage à la vie	*Ode to life*
C'est beau d'avoir élu	It is beautiful to inhabit
Domicile vivant	This living edifice
Et de loger le temps	And to house time
Dans ce cœur continu	In a continuous heartbeat
[…]	[…]
Et d'avoir atteint l'âme	And to have found one's soul
À petits coups de rame	With small strokes of the oar
Pour ne l'effaroucher	To not frighten it
D'une brusque approchée.	With an abrupt approach.
C'est beau d'avoir connu	It is beautiful to have known
L'ombre sous le feuillage	The shadows under the shrubbery
[…]	[…]

It's a lovely poem, with clever rhymes and imagery. However, it loses something in my translation. I love the "soul" part, though I dislike the term "soul." I prefer "authentic self"—it sounds a little less melodramatic.

Perhaps these excerpts from Charles Baudelaire's *Enivrez-vous* (*Get Drunk*) are more accessible:

Original excerpts:	My rough translation:
Enivrez-vous	*Get Drunk*
Il faut être toujours ivre [….]	One must always be drunk […]
Pour ne pas sentir l'horrible fardeau du Temps qui brise vos épaules et vous penche vers la terre, il faut vous enivrer sans trêve.	To not feel the horrible burden of time that breaks your shoulders and forces you down to the ground, one must always get drunk without respite.
Mais de quoi? De vin, de poésie ou de vertu, à votre guise. Mais enivrez-vous.	But on what? On wine, poetry or virtue, whatever you like. But get drunk.
[…]	[…]

Baudelaire isn't endorsing alcoholism. He's promoting a metaphorical inebriation. Get drunk on life, specifically on the things that help you transcend suffering when possible.

I would interpret Baudelaire's mention of "poetry" as meaning the literary arts and probably the creative arts more generally. It could encompass a wider array of interests. There's probably an "art of X" book out there for almost everything: fishing, bird-watching, hiking, bowling, etc.

Virtue likely means helping others in whatever way suits you: recycling, helping an elderly neighbor with her groceries, donating to the local food bank, etc. Of course, his mention of "wine" refers to the more tangible pleasures, such as reveling in good food and drink.

Overall, he's saying, "Why not pursue your passions?" As long as they don't encroach on others' safety and well-being, it makes sense. Not bad advice for a dead, European white guy, right?

And if that still seems too hedonistic for you, Supervielle's advice to pause occasionally to revere beauty throughout your lifespan, despite all life's imperfections and setbacks, is good advice, too.

Acknowledgments

Thanks go to my husband for demonstrating his enthusiasm for this project from day one, and for letting me monopolize the comfy recliner for hours at a time to compulsively type and revise. Thanks also to Jenny for giving me gentle but honest, constructive feedback on my early draft. I am very grateful to the editors and other staff at Luminare Press for patiently and professionally guiding me through this process. Finally, thank you to my Chicago friends, including Kirsten, Kelly, Mary Pat, Olga, and Marcia for your helpful feedback and encouragement during this endeavor.

About the Author

Nina lives in Chicago with her husband and two cats. She works full time as a school-based occupational therapist in the Chicago suburbs. In her spare time, she enjoys hiking, reading, movies, and travel. As of this writing, she has enrolled in an online doctorate program in occupational therapy to advance her expertise and employment options in the field. This is her first nonacademic publication.

www.ingramcontent.com/pod-product-compliance
Lightning Source LLC
LaVergne TN
LVHW092054060526
838201LV00047B/1384